TRANSPARENT FALSEHOOD

An American Travesty

GIL KOFMAN

An up-close, creepily absurd behind-the-scenes
look into Trump's daily life. Never before seen outtakes
invented from a sad overblown life.

PPP PRESS
PicturePendingProductions@gmail.com

TRANSPARENT FALSEHOOD
© Copyright 2018 by Gil Kofman

All rights reserved. This work is fully protected under the copyright laws of the United States of America. No part of this publication may be photocopied, reproduced, stored in a retrieval system, or transmitted, in any form or by any means, electronic, mechanical, recording, or otherwise, without the prior permission of the author or publisher. Additional copies of this play are available from the publisher.

Written permission is required for live performance of any sort. This includes readings, cuttings, scenes, and excerpts. For amateur and stock performances, please contact Picture Pending Productions Press at PicturePendingProductions@gmail.com.

First printing: 2018
ISBN13:9780692138809
(Picture Pending Productions/PPP)
ISBN10:
0692138803

Book design: Jamie Leake
Cover art: Jamie Leake

I love this play. Theatre of the grotesque about one of the most grotesque entities to ever walk the earth. Bold, clever and very funny. But be warned, funny is ugly in this play. And ugly is an incessant reminder of its subject spewing hateful dull-minded nonsense. There is a lot of truth here as well. The kind of truth that sometimes made me want to drown myself in a cold dark lake. Our brave writer has clearly been driven to the edge of madness and is desperately trying (through satire driven by wickedly sharp insight) to claw his way back to some kind of normalcy. We should applaud his valor. Because normalcy has apparently become a vey very difficult place to get to these days. Normalcy is a world where a clown is treated like a clown and the place he inhabits, the ridiculous things he says and does are dismissed as an absurd distraction. Except this clown seems to have found his audience and they don't see him as a clown. They see him as a prophet. And there are way too many of them. Holy shit! Are we in trouble. I think the world (the real one we're losing) needs this play. And maybe a million more of them.

George F. Walker

GIL KOFMAN

Gil Kofman was born in Nigeria. He studied physics at Cornell before attending NYU Graduate Film School, and later receiving an MFA in playwriting from Yale School of Drama. His play *American Magic*, a dark political satire, was produced in NY, LA and London, with Richard Foreman playing the part of the President and original music from Lee Ranaldo. It was later published along with two other plays, *The Interview* and *Pharmacopeia*. His film *The Memory Thief* played on the Sundance Channel. And in 2010 he directed a thriller in China that got a wide release in China and played on HBO Asia. In 2012, he directed and produced a feature film in Tel Aviv called *Lost In The White City* starring Haley Bennett and Thomas Dekker, and was recently a fellow at the MacDowell Colony.

The play premiered in New York City at Theater 511 on April 27, 2018. The cast and creative contributors were:

DONALD J. TRUMP .... Ezra Barnes

BARRON .... Wyatt Fenner

MELANIA TRUMP .... Stephanie Fredricks

IVANKA TRUMP .... Latonia Phipps

STEPHEN BANNON............. Chuck Montgomery

JARED KUSHNER.................... Wyatt Fenner

TEACHER .... Stephanie Fredricks

WRESTLER.................... Chuck Montgomery

TOMMY .... Latonia Phipps (Hand Puppet)

SCHOOL KIDS......... Latonia Phipps (Hand Puppet)

DOCTOR..................... Chuck Montgomery

DAD (FRED TRUMP)............ Stephanie Fredricks

NEWSCASTER #1 . Chuck Montgomery (Hand Puppet)

NEWSCASTER #2 ..... Latonia Phipps (Hand Puppet)

IMMIGRANT ON TV .... Latonia Phipps

DIRECTOR....................... Richard Caliban
SET DESIGN..................... Lianne Arnold
COSTUMES .... Sarah Thea
LIGHTING .... Kia Rogers
STAGE MANAGER .... Blake Kyle

Special Thanks:

Ron Feldman Gallery
for holding a reading of the play on June 8th 2017
as part of their "Art on the Front Lines" show
and Rob Nagle as Trump

CAST
(In Order of Appearance)

DONALD J. TRUMP

BARRON

MELANIA

IVANKA

BANNON

JARED

TEACHER

TOMMY

STUDENT #1

STUDENT #2

STUDENT #3

SECRET SERVICE WRESTLER

DOCTOR

DAD (FRED SR.)

TV ANNOUNCER VOICES

Several roles can be doubled up if needed as follows: BARRON/JARED, IVANKA/TEACHER, BANNON/DAD or any such creative combination. And it's okay for older actors to play BARRON and his fellow students; after all it's theater.

Possible Intermission after Scene 3 and before Scene 4.

PRODUCTION NOTES - TRUMP ON STAGE:

When it came to depicting Trump onstage we were confronted with a salient choice: Do we adhere to the common convention of presenting a Trump who's been infiltrating our minds and dreams 24/7 with a cloying and nauseating abundance - or do we allow theater to carve its own space and interpret Trump as its own. The counter-intuitive choice was to let theater do what it does best - serve as a catalyst for the imagination and the metaphors that thrive there. To do this we thought it was vital to actually hear what Trump was saying and doing beyond the ostentatious and deadening bombast of his ceaseless vapidity, which would have led to a more traditional and congruent casting and style than we chose to embrace. Instead we ignored Trump's signature comportment, age and physical bearing, we overlooked the ethnicity of certain family members, as well as double cast gender in some roles for specific effects. Our aim was to italicize and reclaim what was lost in all the white noise of Trump's thoughtless chaos. To make an active choice not to contribute to that confusion but stand outside it in some signal relief, and revisit the Trump phenomenon so we could finally digest the ongoing horror with something other than disposable outrage. Doing otherwise felt pointless and superfluous: one might just as well turn on the tv or radio, check twitter and various news feeds -where one calamity was so swiftly displacing another we couldn't even grieve properly for the ongoing erosion and destruction of self-evident truths we took for granted. And so we preferred to err on the side of less Trump is more - to remove him from the overtly political sphere, and provide his portrayal with a touch of novelty that offered us a renewed and poignant passport into the enveloping madness. Maybe it's too soon for this kind of treatment, I'm not sure, but living eclipsed in Trump's shadow part of me felt it was more than warranted, if not an actual antidote to his vampiric all-consuming narcissism.

TRANSPARENT FALSEHOOD

1

AS YOUR FATHER AND PRESIDENT

<u>Scene:</u> *Trump is putting his son Barron to bed. Telling him a story. He plays a game where Barron lays his hands in Trump's tiny hands, who tries to slap them before Barron can pull them away.*

                BARRON
Would they really cut my head off?

             DONALD J. TRUMP
Like slicing a piece of white bread.

                BARRON
I'm scared.

DONALD J. TRUMP
Then they'd butter it with your blood instead of jam and eat it.

BARRON
You're really scaring me dad.

DONALD J. TRUMP
These are bad people. Bad *hombres* who live in a *huuuge* desert, with lots of oil that by all rights should be ours. And they'll do anything to stop us. Anything.

BARRON
Stop.

DONALD J. TRUMP
Don't be a sissy, Barron. Only losers get scared.

Trump slaps the shit out of his hand.

BARRON
Dad, how do I know I'm not a loser?

DONALD J. TRUMP
You can't be a loser. You're my son.
  (He extends his hands.)
Again?
  (Barron places them in Trump's palms)
But I admit, it's not a fun way to go. Although as your father and President it's my duty to tell you the truth. Usually, they like to slice the head off with a very dull rusty knife, and do it very very slowly, smiling the whole time, slicing from ear to ear. Back and forth like this. Then they hold up your dripping

head so it can gaze at the headless body that was once part of it before you lose consciousness. So there you are staring at your own headless body while someone else is holding your cut-off head. Not a great feeling. Last thing to look at. Your own lifeless body. Not very Christian.

BARRON
Do they also kill kids?

DONALD J. TRUMP
Oh yeah. They love killing kids. Love the carnage. Kids. Babies. Pets. They don't care. These are bad bad people. That's why I'm trying to keep them out.

BARRON
But why would they do that, Dad?

DONALD J. TRUMP *(shrugs)*
Muslim. Why else?

Again he nails Barron, slapping his hands raw. Barron tries not to cry. Suddenly points at curtains and shrieks.

BARRON
Ahhhh!

DONALD J. TRUMP
What? WHAT?!

BARRON
Can you check behind the curtains for me. I think there's someone there.

DONALD J. TRUMP
Not here. Daddy's made sure they can't come here. Not this room. Not this country.

BARRON
But I saw the curtains move.

DONALD J. TRUMP
That must be the breeze. Or my camera crew.

BARRON
Camera crew? Really? You mean for TV?

DONALD J. TRUMP
They're very good at hiding and concealing themselves. The best. But *shhh* no one's suppose to know. You know how people are when they get before cameras. I want this to be all natural. Nothing fake. All real.

BARRON
You're not just saying that so I won't be scared.

DONALD J. TRUMP
As President *and* your *dad*, I've always got a camera crew now. So I get to tell the truth as it needs to be told. Without all this *fake* media around me. I want people to know the real me. So they can feel closer… better connected… and reject all the fake dishonest news. The news has been very unfair about your father.

BARRON
I'm sorry dad. I'm sorry so many people don't like you.

DONALD J. TRUMP
People don't always know what's good for them. That's what the show is about tonight. The theater. My HBO Special. This crew. I've gotten rid of all the dishonest and nasty press conferences. From now on it's going to be *my* press. *My* crew.

BARRON *(looking towards curtains)*
Can I see them?

DONALD J. TRUMP
Maybe later. *(Beat)* Now your mom tells me you got into a bit of trouble at school. Just like your father.

BARRON
They said I cheated on my test.

DONALD J. TRUMP
Did you?

BARRON
I hate math.

DONALD J. TRUMP
You might hate it, but you need to know your math. Helps with the business, you know. Especially multiplication. Much more important than division. Division is for losers. How much you lost. You divide. It's like subtraction in big handfuls. But multiplication is different. You want to know your multiplication tables. That's important stuff.

TRANSPARENT FALSEHOOD

BARRON
I'm having a hard time memorizing them, Dad.

DONALD J. TRUMP
Ok, that's ok. Just eyeball it. That's what I often do. You *guess-timate*. As long as you can eye things it's good enough. Sometimes the guess is as good as the math. Or even better. For example what's 300,000 times 10.

BARRON
I don't know.

DONALD J. TRUMP
Think.
(Barron shrugs)
Ok, I'll give you a hint. Because you're my son and it's time for bed. I'll give you a small *guesstimation* hint. How many people were are my inauguration? Remember that….?

BARRON
The news said it-

DONALD J. TRUMP *(exploding)*
Forget the news!! News knows shit. Fake. Phony. Dishonest. Trust your eyes. What you saw.

BARRON
I….

DONALD J. TRUMP
At least 3 million.

            BARRON
Really?

            DONALD J. TRUMP
Would I lie to you?

            BARRON
No, dad.

            DONALD J. TRUMP
More people than the naked eye could see. Largest inauguration ceremony in history. More than their love could hold. Sun coming out and stopping the rain as it fell. Raindrops suspended mid-air. Amazing. The sea of faces. That's affection. Love. I'll never forget it. I'll tell you a secret. As your father and President, can I share a little secret with you? In my dreams… all those faces, the multitude of millions that were there to welcome me - they all had plastic surgery so they could look like me. All their faces identical to mine. Happy to make America great again. What do you dream about son…?

            BARRON
I want to fly Air Force one.

            DONALD J. TRUMP
That's your dream.

            BARRON
Yes.

TRANSPARENT FALSEHOOD

> DONALD J. TRUMP
>
> Done! You pass your math and I'll make sure you get to go into the cockpit and fly Air Force One all day.

> BARRON
>
> Can I also hold the "football"?

> DONALD J. TRUMP
>
> Um. You know, son, that' s not a *real* football, it's just what they call it.

> BARRON
>
> I know. I know. Can I hold it. It would be soooo cool.

> DONALD J. TRUMP
>
> I'll see what I can do. Now did you or didn't you cheat on that math exam?

> BARRON
>
> No.

> DONALD J. TRUMP
>
> Not that there's anything wrong with cheating.

> BARRON
>
> I didn't cheat, dad.

> DONALD J. TRUMP
>
> Not if you don't get caught.

> BARRON
>
> I didn't —

                    DONALD J. TRUMP
Are you lying to me?

                    BARRON
No.

                    DONALD J. TRUMP
You sure?

                    BARRON
A… little.

                    DONALD J. TRUMP
Little what…?

                    BARRON
I might have cheated a little tiny bit. I'm sorry.

                    DONALD J. TRUMP
Hey! What have I taught you? What have I taught you?!

                    BARRON
Big. Always lie big.

                    DONALD J. TRUMP
The bigger the better.

                    BARRON
Like when we played golf together and you moved your ball?

DONALD J. TRUMP *(defensive)*
What are you talking about?

BARRON
Don't worry I won't tell anyone, Dad.

DONALD J. TRUMP *(vicious)*
There's nothing to tell. You are just a boy. No one will believe you anyway.

BARRON
But....

DONALD J. TRUMP *(impatient, deflecting)*
So what else are they teaching you in school? Tell me.

BARRON
Cursive handwriting.

DONALD J. TRUMP
They still teach that? A waste. No merit.

BARRON
They said we need to know it so we can sign our names.

DONALD J. TRUMP
Oh well, that's true. Good point. When you take over the family Empire, um, I mean... business, you'll need to sign a lot of things.
(hands him the presidential I-Cross pen)
Here. It's yours.

BARRON

Wow dad!

DONALD J. TRUMP

I signed some of my best Executive Orders with this.

BARRON

It's got your name on it.

DONALD J. TRUMP

In gold!

BARRON

Can't wait till I bring it to school.

DONALD J. TRUMP

You use that on your test and no one will say anything. Trust me. You can cheat as much as you want with *that* pen. Now let me see you sign your name.

BARRON

I don't have any paper…

Donald hands him a check.

DONALD J. TRUMP

Here. You sign this… check. *One Million Dollars!* A little whore money for when you get older, but don't tell your mom.

They High Five.

BARRON

You're the best dad.

DONALD J. TRUMP

Now, sign. That's it. Put some more *oomph* into it.

As he signs his name. Admires it.

BARRON

Where did my name come from Dad?

DONALD J. TRUMP

Barron? Um… an old family name. On my mom's Scottish side. You remember *Braveheart* with Mel Gibson trying to make Scotland great again? That movie was based on our family story. If you notice, Mel had very similar hair to me in that movie, only much longer. *Girlish*. A real winner. That movie. Not William Wallace haha. He was captured. Tortured. Killed. But that movie won Five Academy awards. *Five! (Beat)* Now let me see that check.

He inspects the freshly signed Million Dollar check.

BARRON

How much is a million dollars?

DONALD J. TRUMP

Depends on the quality of porn star you want to buy. Just kidding. I'm in a crazy mood tonight. You're dad is craaaazy. Because he has his show to go to. Very big deal.

Melania's Voice from Offstage.

MELANIA *(OS)*
Donald! We have to leave. Secret service just buzzed from downstairs.

DONALD J. TRUMP *(back to her)*
Ignore them. We've got the motorcade, hon. Relax. We can cut right through traffic.

BARRON
Are you going to come home late?

DONALD J. TRUMP
Not sure. Depends how great the show goes.

BARRON
Mommy says it's a presidential one-man HBO special.

DONALD J. TRUMP
Yes it is. And I bet it gets the highest rating they've ever had.

BARRON
More than *girls*?

DONALD J. TRUMP
Puhleasse! I hope you don't watch that stuff. It'll shrink your dick. I'm serious. That show should be called *PIGS*. I'd rather get blown in a Turkish bathhouse than watch that garbage. You know, son, there's a reason they invented the radio, so you don't have to watch crap like that.

BARRON
What about your special though? Can I watch that?

DONALD J. TRUMP
Sure. I'll get you a tape. But you have to go to sleep now or dad's gonna be super late and the whole thing'll be cancelled.

BARRON
Will you come home right after?

DONALD J. TRUMP
Sure. If I don't have to save the world. World is a mess, son. And I might have to save it. A real mess they left me.

BARRON
But you'll come home after.

DONALD J. TRUMP
Sure. When I'm done, I'll be home.

BARRON
You're not lying to me again?

DONALD J. TRUMP
Would The Big Donald lie to The Little Donald?

Barron doesn't answer. Pause.

BARRON
I just want you to be here when I wake up.

DONALD J. TRUMP
Of course, of course I will. Now I really gotta go. I've got what they call a… *curtain call.*

BARRON
Dad!

Donald stops, turns. "What now?"

BARRON
Can mom stay here with me tonight if you can't?

DONALD J. TRUMP
No can do. Part of being a powerful man means having a beautiful woman on your arm. And your mom, well… she can be quite a hooker under the right light…

BARRON
Mom's not a hooker!

DONALD J. TRUMP *(overlap)*
I said *looker*, Barron, *looker!*

BARRON
But some kids at school said—

DONALD J. TRUMP
You're just tired. Go to sleep.

BARRON
How did you and mom meet?
(Trump hesitates telling)
Please.

DONALD J. TRUMP
Prima Nocta.

BARRON
What's that?

DONALD J. TRUMP
When you see *Braveheart* you'll understand. Now you really want to know why I married your mom?

BARRON
Because you love her?

DONALD J. TRUMP
Yeah, sure, guess again.

BARRON
Because she's so beautiful?

DONALD J. TRUMP
She was. Yes. When I married her.

BARRON
She still is dad.

DONALD J. TRUMP
Sure sure. But you want to know why I *really* married your mother?

BARRON
Why, Dad…?

DONALD J. TRUMP
Cause I couldn't marry Ivanka. That's why.

                    BARRON
Ewww. Ivanka is your daughter.

                DONALD J. TRUMP
Exactly.

                    BARRON
You can't marry your own daughter.

                DONALD J. TRUMP
Of course not. Think I don't know that. Some lies are too big league even for me. That's how they become taboos.

Offstage Melania calls again.

                    MELANIA
Donald!

                DONALD J. TRUMP
One minute!

                    BARRON
You really in the Wrestling Hall of Fame, Dad.

                DONALD J. TRUMP
Nice try, kid. You know I am.

                    BARRON
Sorry, dad.

                DONALD J. TRUMP
Here. I'll show you the duck under before I go.

As he wrestles Barron and pins him on the bed, he notices a large bruise.

                DONALD J. TRUMP
Hey what's this?

                BARRON
Nothing.

                DONALD J. TRUMP
You know you can tell me anything.

                BARRON
I know.

                DONALD J. TRUMP
You have to tell me everything. *(Silence)* I'm not only your dad. I'm also your President. I can waterboard you, you know.

                BARRON *(to Melania offstage)*
Mommy!! Dad is threatening to waterboard me again.

                MELANIA *(O.S.)*
Donald!

                DONALD J. TRUMP *(to Barron)*
I can't believe you just snitched on me to your mother like that.

                BARRON
Next time I'll call my lawyer.

DONALD J. TRUMP
Nice!

They high five again.

DONALD J. TRUMP *(re bruise)*
So. Tell me. What happened?

BARRON
I told you dad, nothing –

He examines Barron's upper arm.

DONALD J. TRUMP
You've got a good bruise on your arm. That's a black and blue mark. I've been married 3 times, I know a bruise when I see one.

Long pause.

BARRON
I already told you… they called mom some names.

DONALD J. TRUMP
Really…? Mom…? *(slight disappointment)* Nothing about me!?

BARRON
No dad, this had nothing to do with you.

MELANIA *(O.S.)*
Donald, theater just called. They want to know if we're on our way.

DONALD J. TRUMP
Go on, son. Tell me. *(pause, more sinister)* Barron, tell me!

Donald twists Barron's arm.

BARRON
You are hurting me.

DONALD J. TRUMP
Tell me what they said.

Barron leans in to whisper.

BARRON
They called Mom a… *(inaudible whisper)*

DONALD J. TRUMP
No…

BARRON
Is it true?

DONALD J. TRUMP
Does it matter? People like to say things about other people all the time. The more rich and good looking they are, the more people talk.

BARRON
They showed me photos on their phone.

DONALD J. TRUMP
Who?

BARRON
Some of the kids.

DONALD J. TRUMP
I want their names. And parents names.

BARRON
But—

DONALD J. TRUMP
Also your Teacher's name.

BARRON
But is it true…?

DONALD J. TRUMP
How can you even ask? Fake news. All of it. That's why I'm doing my HBO show. This documentary film. Recording everything that's going on.

BARRON
So it's a lie. About mother?

DONALD J. TRUMP
Of course, son, of course.

Melania enters.

MELANIA
How are we doing in here? All ready for a kiss Little Donald?

She leans in to kiss Barron, as Donald gropes her.

DONALD J. TRUMP
No tongue, Melania.

MELANIA
You are disgusting.

BARRON
I love you Mommy, Daddy.

MELANIA
We love you too but we will be late for theater. And your father is star tonight.

DONALD J. TRUMP
Every night!

MELANIA
Big star on broadway show.

BARRON
Can you read me a little before you go? Please. I'm still scared.

MELANIA
Has Donald been telling you bad stories again?

DONALD J. TRUMP
I just want him to be prepared for the world... the *carnage*.

MELANIA
Not smart, Donald. Not before we go out. No common sense this one.

BARRON
Just a little story. Something to undo the bad ones. Something nice.

DONALD J. TRUMP
The audience can wait a little longer. More they wait, the more appreciative they'll be.

MELANIA
You're the boss.

DONALD J. TRUMP
That's right I am.

MELANIA
I'll do a little more hair.

DONALD J. TRUMP
A few sit-ups won't hurt either.

She exits room. He reaches for a book.

DONALD J. TRUMP
Ok. Now I'm going to read you from my all time favorite and best book.

BARRON
The Bible…?

DONALD J. TRUMP
Better. "The Art of the Deal". Great book. You guys reading it in class yet.

BARRON
No.

DONALD J. TRUMP
Why not?

Barron shrugs.

DONALD J. TRUMP
This should be part of every curriculum. Everywhere. They can teach you math and chemistry and history all day long, but nothing's as important as *making a deal*. You know that… right?

BARRON
Yes, dad.

DONALD J. TRUMP
If you can make a deal, you'll never go hungry.
   (prepares to read from Art of the Deal.)
Anyone can teach a man to fish, but if you can teach him to make a *deal*, he'll never have to fish again.

BARRON
Why not?

DONALD J. TRUMP
Because he can always take someone else's fish!

                    BARRON
What if you don't like fish?

                DONALD J. TRUMP
You can substitute whatever you want. You like pizza?

                    BARRON
Yessss.

                DONALD J. TRUMP
With the *Art of the Deal,* you can trade things for pizza.

                    BARRON
But nobody fishes for pizza.

            DONALD J. TRUMP *(impatient)*
You want me to read or not?

                    BARRON
Please.

He cracks open "Art of the Deal".

                DONALD J. TRUMP
I think you'll find this passage very fitting. Given your current school situation, I think this might speak to you.
   (He clears his throat to read, Barron listens. Reads.)
"Even in elementary school, I was a very assertive, aggressive kid. In the 2nd grade I actually gave a teacher a black eye—"

                    BARRON
You did...?!

                    DONALD J. TRUMP *(continues reading)*
"- I punched my music teacher because I didn't think he knew anything about music."

                    BARRON
Wow, you're so cool dad.

                    DONALD J. TRUMP
I know.

                    MELANIA *(O.S.)*
Donald! Please.

                    DONALD J. TRUMP
I'm coming. *(to Barron)* Go to sleep. Love you son.

                    BARRON
Mmmm. Love you too dad.

Donald heads to door, stops to address imaginary film crew.

                    DONALD J. TRUMP
You guys coming or what?

2

AS YOUR HUSBAND AND PRESIDENT

<u>Scene:</u> - *Trump and Melania get ready for their big theater night. He's texting and knotting his tie. TV in background.*

DONALD J. TRUMP
How do you like my tie?

MELANIA
Does it matter what I think?

DONALD J. TRUMP
No. You're right. It doesn't.

He knots tie.

MELANIA
Zip me up.

DONALD J. TRUMP
Do it yourself.

She struggles to zip up.

MELANIA
Is he going to be ok?

DONALD J. TRUMP
Who… Barron?

MELANIA
This might be too much for him.

DONALD J. TRUMP
Ok, I'll quit. I'll give up being president to take care of my 11 year old. Are you crazy…?

MELANIA
It's just so much for him to process, Donald.

DONALD J. TRUMP
You baby him too much. Too much. Not good.

MELANIA
Some people need that more than others.

DONALD J. TRUMP
You'll make him soft. It's a hard world. You know that. Hard. Mean. My father never babied me like that.

MELANIA
And look what happen to your brother, Fred.

DONALD J. TRUMP
Exactly why you have to be tough. Hard. My brother Fred was too soft. Sentimental. Never show what's inside. Better yet - never have anything inside to show.

MELANIA
I want our child to be happy. Is that so wrong?

DONALD J. TRUMP
And I want him to be a man. Like his father.

MELANIA *(pointed)*
No. Little Donald, will never be like you.

DONALD J. TRUMP
Not if you keep coddling him. Does he still nurse?

MELANIA
Donald!

DONALD J. TRUMP
I don't know. Some cultures do, you know. Of course you never hear about them. Why would you. I'm sure they are all too busy sucking on Momma's tits for you to hear about them or their achievements.

He makes a rude noise with his lips.

MELANIA
I just worry about him. You see the way he is…

DONALD J. TRUMP
And you're only making it worse. I think you should stay here tonight. With your baby Barron.

MELANIA
But I want to be there for your big night, Donald.

DONALD J. TRUMP
I'm sure you do.

MELANIA
Please Donald.

DONALD J. TRUMP
You can watch me on TV, I'm always on tv now. If only there was a way to get residuals for all my appearances. Maybe I can sign an Executive Order to change that. Why should these sonofbitches benefit from my appearance.

MELANIA
Don't make me stay Donald. Please. I want to-

DONALD J. TRUMP
Don't think so. You can be quite a liability you know. It's not just tonight. That look on your face. When I got elected. Always suffering. Who needs that? That "bitch face" has got to go now that you're First Lady.

MELANIA
It's just too much, Donald, all at once. I think people don't like me.

DONALD J. TRUMP
Is that what this is? About you? YOU?!

MELANIA
Shhh, you'll wake up Barron.

DONALD J. TRUMP
Fuck Barron! Who out there will trade places with you when the firing squad comes. No one. Being *liked* is overrated. You can get better ratings for being *disliked* than being *liked*.

He ups the volume on TV News. ANNOUNCER'S VOICE.

TV ANNOUNCER #1
So if Trump rejects DACA and deports millions of illegal immigrants, my question is, who would be left to build his wall?

Trump angrily switches channel.

DONALD J. TRUMP
Wait and see. Wait and see.

TV ANNOUNCER #2
On a lighter note, we found one clever traveler who manages to enter the country without much trouble. What's your secret. Isn't your country on the disputed travel ban?

TRANSPARENT FALSEHOOD

Camera cuts to an immigrant WOMAN on Camera.

MARIA *(accented)*
Every time I travel, I just make sure to dress up and wear everything from the Ivanka Trump line, including her perfume. Shoes. Purse. They let me right through.

DONALD J. TRUMP
See, Melania! There's a resourceful person. Why can't other immigrants be like that. Why can't they just let me do my work.

MELANIA
I don't know, honey. Genius is often misunderstood.

DONALD J. TRUMP
I love when you call me that. Come here.

She goes to him reluctantly as he starts to paw her brusquely.

MELANIA
Not now, Donald.

DONALD J. TRUMP
Why not. I need this. For my show. To clear my head. You'll be putting out for the good of the country.

He increases his assault. An animal without a trace of tenderness.

Another report comes in as he assaults her.

TV ANNOUNCER #2

Another Russian diplomat was found dead tonight from an apparent heart attack. It seems that more Russian diplomats have dropped dead since Trump's inauguration than in the past eight years with Obama. In light of previous findings, officials say an autopsy will certainly be conducted.

DONALD J. TRUMP

I suppose they'll be blaming me for that!

He continues to inflict himself on Melania. Humping harder.

MELANIA

Please Donald. Slower. You're hurting me.

DONALD J. TRUMP

I want you to feel me.

MELANIA

I feel you.

DONALD J. TRUMP

My power.

MELANIA

Yes.

DONALD J. TRUMP

My strength.

TRANSPARENT FALSEHOOD

MELANIA
Yes. Yes.

DONALD J. TRUMP
See hon, I'm everywhere. Inside you. On TV. Everywhere!

TV ANNOUNCER #3 *(overlapping w/ above)*
I tell you, they must be feeling the heat. Each day, the Trump-Russia connection appears to be more clearly drawn and closing in. We should be seeing a critical mass very soon.

DONALD J. TRUMP
(As he continues pounding/raping Melania, rabidly changing channels.)
Puhleaseee! They exaggerate everything. Even my exaggerations are exaggerated! I've never lied to them. Not the people. How I dress it up is my business. The message has always been the same. Always!
(thrusting violently)
Am I lying now? Am I lying now??! Who's lying now?! WHO'S LYING NOW?!

He finishes with Melania, pushing her away. Switches off TV in disgust. Then zips up and arranges himself.

DONALD J. TRUMP
They want answers, I'll give them answers. I'll deliver a truth that won't be questioned. Can't be questioned. Between this new HBO special and my new exposé documentary, I'll show everyone what's fake and not. *(He turns to the wings)* Right guys?

MELANIA *(looks about)*
Who are you talking to?

DONALD J. TRUMP
My crew.
   (Melania stares at him, incredulous, bewildered.)
My camera crew.

MELANIA
Where?

DONALD J. TRUMP
You're looking right at them.

MELANIA
I don't see anyone.

DONALD J. TRUMP
Of course you don't. If you did they wouldn't be doing their job. They're professionals. The best money can buy. *(misusing the word)* Incognito.

MELANIA
They might be incognito, but why can't I see them?

DONALD J. TRUMP
Like a fly on the wall. They're following my every move. Now I love the First Amendment, no one loves it more than me. But I'm done with the Opposition. Abolish the Press. You know what Jefferson said about the press, the pollution – *(off her look)* – no, why would you? You're just a dumb immigrant. You don't even know who Jefferson was…? Hey

guys, come out here and meet FLOTUS.
(He introduces her to an invisible crew that's not there.)
Clive here is doing sound. Great guy. Top in his field. African American too. Right here brother!
(He gives an invisible hi-5 to Clive)
And people call me racist. I'm the least racist person I know. Oh, and this here's Al, he's doing camera… so you want to get on his good side, if you know what I mean. And last but not least there's Paul, - Paul is the director-slash-producer of this whole *shebang*. Although I'm the real producer. Go on say hi.

She reluctantly, meekly, says Hi to invisible crew.

    MELANIA *(diffident)*
Hi.

    DONALD J. TRUMP
Hey guys, stop staring at Melania's tits. She's first lady now. Show some respect.

They all laugh and fist bump - Donald and the invisible crew.

    MELANIA *(tentatively, concerned)*
Where did you find them Donald?

    DONALD J. TRUMP
Bannon used them on his documentaries, loves them. Said Paul, the director, he's like the Leni Reifensthal of our times. I said why not Lucas or Coppola, why does it have to be a woman.

MELANIA *(simmering)*
Were they in Barron's room?

DONALD J. TRUMP
Smart boy. He knew someone was there. Sensed it.

MELANIA
I thought we agree to keep Barron out of this.

DONALD J. TRUMP
There you go babying him again.

MELANIA
He's only a boy.

DONALD J. TRUMP
I'm sorry, but nothing is off limits. I'm covering everything here. Otherwise they'll say I'm hiding things. You know the Opposition. How they are. Donald Trump is inventing again. Fabricating. Donald Trump gilds the truth with lies.
(Motions to film crew.)
I even tell them my dreams. Don't I...? I tell them everything.
(Smiles. Back to Melania, for Camera.)
Remember how we first met? New York Fashion week.

She looks down.

DONALD J. TRUMP *(gestures to Camera Crew)*
Go on, tell them the story. Great story.

MELANIA

Please, Donald, you'll be so late. You hate being late.

DONALD J. TRUMP

Let me worry about that. Tell them how we met… what you first said to me.

MELANIA

I don't remember.

DONALD J. TRUMP

Sure you do. Melania was here in the country on a special visa awarded only to those showing "extraordinary gifts" and talent in their chosen profession.

MELANIA

Yes, it is true. They give me visa for my extraordinary gifts.

DONALD J. TRUMP

Madame Curie, Albert Einstein…. and now Melania Trump. Go on, hon, show them your great talents. How you got into this great country in the first place.

MELANIA

Please no Donald. It embarrasses me.

DONALD J. TRUMP

She's so modest. Walk down the runway. Shake your ass a bit. *(to camera guy)* Make sure to have them zoom in slowly, Paul. *(smacks her ass)* Go on.

Melania reluctantly paces back and forth.

DONALD J. TRUMP

Ewww. Not at all like I remember it. She used to have such a great ass. So sad.

MELANIA

Please stop…

DONALD J. TRUMP

Used to be so amazing. If only you could've seen her in her day. Not like now. Retired to pasture. Very sad. Trying so hard to be respectable. Looking after women's issues, kids welfare, cyberbullying. Nothing compared to how she was back then. So unbelievably hot. The way she walked down the runway. And it made me so hot. And I had to meet her. And I did. And on the first date I asked her if she was only attracted to me only because I was so successful and fabulously rich - and she answered… go on, tell them.

MELANIA

I said:

DONALD J. TRUMP *(sharp reprimand)*

Over there! What are you doing? Talk to the camera. Camera is over there! Where are you looking at you dumb cow?!

MELANIA

Sorry.

She re-orients herself in room. Addressing invisible Camera Crew.

    DONALD J. TRUMP *(sweet again)*
Tell them what you said.

    MELANIA
I said: "You might be rich and successful but if I weren't so beautiful, do you think you'd still be here talking to me?"

    DONALD J. TRUMP
Touché, I laughed. Then she took my hand and placed it between her thighs, said: *I feel like…*

    MELANIA *(completing)*
…Cinderella.

    DONALD J. TRUMP
You hear that guys…? *Cinderella.*

    MELANIA
Although you have small hands, I said, *I have a feeling you'll make a perfect fit.*

    DONALD J. TRUMP
- and I had to literally shoehorn my penis into the tight garage of her vagina.

    MELANIA
Donald!

DONALD J. TRUMP
But we made it work. Pornstars notwithstanding we made it work. And there was no #MeToo nonsense with the Trumpster. Just MeMeME!
(Beat)
Now look at her. Awful. Such short shelf life. Sad unhappy tits.

MELANIA
Don't be cruel, Donald.

DONALD J. TRUMP
Hey, my testicles aren't that happy either. But I'm 30 years older. And I am the President.

MELANIA
Not for ever.

DONALD J. TRUMP
Are you trying to curse me? You cold Slavic witch?

MELANIA
Of course not, Donald, but things they change.

DONALD J. TRUMP
You bet they do. I used to run Miss Universe for years. I've seen change up close and it ain't pretty. Way your tits sag now. So sad. Practically weeping. You've got sobbing tits. You are no longer the 10 you were when I met you. It happens. That's life, babe. Time to move on. Which means, you shouldn't be wearing dresses like that anymore.

MELANIA
What's wrong with my dress? You bought it for me.

DONALD J. TRUMP
You really want me to say?
(gestures to Camera Crew)
In front of them?

Doorbell rings. Donald shoves Melania out of the way.

DONALD J. TRUMP
Excuse me.

MELANIA
Are you expecting someone? Who are you—

Ivanka enters brightly.

IVANKA
Daddy!

DONALD J. TRUMP
Hello favorite and "chosen one". How are you…?

IVANKA
You ready for your big show, Daddy?

MELANIA
She's going to show?!

IVANKA
Wouldn't miss it for the world. Aren't you coming?

MELANIA
I want to but the Donald-

DONALD J. TRUMP *(overlap)*
She can't. *(whispers)* Barron.

IVANKA
Ah.

DONALD J. TRUMP *(to Ivanka)*
Come on, hon. It's opening night.

MELANIA
Wait. Isn't it the holy Sabbath for your people.

IVANKA
Snuck out when Jared was praying.

DONALD J. TRUMP
You sure he didn't see you?

IVANKA
They separate the men and women anyway.

DONALD J. TRUMP
These Jews, haha. Better at counting shekels than their women. How's your math these days? Now that you converted?

IVANKA
I don't know. Ok I guess.

DONALD J. TRUMP
Good. I need you to tutor Barron. Kid's kind of weak with his arithmetic. Think you could do that?

IVANKA
Sure. Anything for you, daddy.

DONALD J. TRUMP
My Ivanka… even smarter now that she's a Jew.

MELANIA *(accusatory)*
Is that why you asked me to stay home. To go out alone. With your little Ivanka?

DONALD J. TRUMP
Of course not. I was thinking of Barron. And your cyberbullying platform. Love what you can do with that. Helping children all over. So much to do. So many good things. I can tweet about it if you want. Make sure people get behind you or they'll get shamed in public.

IVANKA
But that would be bullying, dad.

DONALD J. TRUMP
Not if it's for a good cause you believe in.

MELANIA
Thanks, but I'll manage on my own.

IVANKA
Speaking of bullying… what's with the security downstairs?

                    DONALD J. TRUMP
Why? What's wrong with it?

                         IVANKA
Nothing. Just sucks. Can't believe we're paying for that incompetence.

                    DONALD J. TRUMP
Actually… I got the public to pay for it.

                        MELANIA
Your father is very good that way.

                         IVANKA
You should fire them anyway. This one guard, might have been Latino, not sure. *Definitely* brown. He tried to stop me and put his dirty hands on my shoulder, here, and got some burrito he was eating all over my dress.

                    DONALD J. TRUMP
You get his name?

                         IVANKA
No.

Melania approaches with some club soda.

                        MELANIA
Here try this. Should work with stain.

                    DONALD J. TRUMP
I'll check the security cameras and find out who it was.

Ivanka tries to remove stain. It doesn't come off.

IVANKA
I can't go out like this Daddy. Your big night. What if the press takes photos. You know they'll make the stain bigger in photoshop, those liars. My line of clothing is already hurting. They'll just make a meal of this.

DONALD J. TRUMP
The press are heartless. A stain on everything. Not just your dress.

Melania still rubbing.

IVANKA *(to Melania)*
Ugh, you're only making it worse.

DONALD J. TRUMP
I've got a brilliant idea.

IVANKA
You always do, Daddy.

DONALD J. TRUMP
Melania… give Ivanka your dress.

MELANIA
But—

DONALD J. TRUMP
Do as your told. I'm not only your husband but also your President now. Besides, I told you, you're too old to wear that. Come on.

Melania strips, Donald winces at sight of her body.

> IVANKA

Thanks Melania.

Melania reluctantly hands her dress to Ivanka.

> DONALD J. TRUMP

You really need to up your aerobics, babe, this is an insult. You're the first lady now. Look at Ivanka. Her body.

Melania puts on a bathrobe.

> IVANKA

I'm so excited, Daddy. Obama did HBO, but never like you. Not a one-man show!!

> DONALD J. TRUMP

No one's done what I'm doing. I'm the first. Ever. In the whole history. Donald J. Trump is - "Without Precedent".

> IVANKA

Great title dad.

> DONALD J. TRUMP

I know. *(Hands across the air)* WITHOUT PRECEDENT.

> MELANIA

Just make sure they spell it right this time, Donald.

> DONALD J. TRUMP

Don't be negative. Always so negative, this one. Must be that cold Eastern European thing.

MELANIA
But they spelled it wrong last time. *WITHOUT PRESIDENT.* Remember how upset you were. Once I pointed it out.

IVANKA
How long is the show?

DONALD J. TRUMP
Depends… I'm going to improv most of it. Best prep is no prep. Keeps it fresh. *REAL!!*

IVANKA
You're so good at that dad.

DONALD J. TRUMP
Going to be a great crowd. Great crowd. Lines around the block.

IVANKA
Are they filming it?

DONALD J. TRUMP
Yes. But I'm bringing my own crew as well.

IVANKA
Your own…?

DONALD J. TRUMP
Think I trust anyone else?

MELANIA
Bannon introduced them to him.

IVANKA

Really.

DONALD J. TRUMP

Melania loved them. Didn't you hon?

She smiles coldly.

IVANKA

Are they already setting up?

DONALD J. TRUMP

Oh no. They're here. All around us. Want to meet them?

IVANKA

Here…?

MELANIA

Donald says they're like Ninja.

DONALD J. TRUMP

She doesn't even know what a Ninja is.

IVANKA

Maybe later. We're already late. *(to Melania)* Can you zip me up?

DONALD J. TRUMP

Let me do that, babe. *(He zips up Ivanka's dress. Turns to Melania)* You stay here and do some sit ups. Go on, start your sit ups. Now.

IVANKA
Ooo, I love the tie Dad. Soooo you.
> *(to Melania on the floor doing sit ups.)*

Daddy is going to set the world straight. Clean up the mess he inherited. So everyone loves him as much as I do.

DONALD J. TRUMP
That can never be. No one loves me like you.

MELANIA
But people, they try. They learn.

DONALD J. TRUMP
Quiet! And do your crunches.

Melania continues her sullen sit-ups as Ivanka steps over her.

IVANKA
Come on Daddy. We don't want to be too late.

3

AS LEADING MAN
AND YOUR PRESIDENT

<u>Scene:</u> *Empty stage. Loud raucous applause. It goes on and on. Grows louder as fog and haze fill the stage and a silhouetted figure in a long coat appears. He stands and waves. Applause crescendos to the tune of Queen's "We Are the Champions".*

More waving, more applause. The American flag is projected across back of theater, as the figure steps forward and lights shift to reveal Donald J. Trump. Clapping along, playing to audience.

He raises his hand. Silence descends. He waits. Teases Audience.

DONALD J. TRUMP

Tonight I want to talk about theater. Yes theater. Tonight is about about you. *You* the *People.* And *Making Theater Great Again.*

More applause.

DONALD J. TRUMP

Tonight is about you and me here in this room. No ugly politics. The terrible witch hunts, the lying press. Russia. China. The unfair Paris *Dis*-Agreement. Health care. Taxes. Immigrants. Dreamers. No. Tonight is my message of pure love.

More applause.

DONALD J. TRUMP

Come on, sounds like death out there. *(Listens.)* Louder! Clap *loud* or people will say you sound like Democrats. Un-American! Treasonous!

Louder applause. He drinks it in.

Now I'm not sure how many of you know this, but when I was preparing to come into office in January - and it wasn't easy, *I didn't need to do this,* but I *wanted* to do it, for *you,* the *people* - when I came into office in January, Ringling Bros and Barnum Bailey were on their sad way out. After 146 years of running an incredible business, with incredible acts, stuff I remember seeing with my dad as a kid, great man my dad, good guy, not just because he took me to the circus, but all his other accomplishments, so great!
    (He looks up to Heavens)
Remember that one time we went to the circus Dad and we saw those skinny women swallowing those long swords, wow, amazing people, hardworking, but now it's time for failing Ringling Bros to end their show and

make room for someone else. There can be only *ONE Greatest Showman on Earth* at a time. That's the *1st Rule* of theater. So they had to close shop and make room for The Donald. But we will remember them forever. Won't we? Put up quite a fight. But in the end there can be only one winner. And I promise you you won't regret the *new* improved act with the *new* greatest showman in history - DONALD J. TRUMP. Forget the three ring circus. We're talking at least a *thousand rings* here! Stuff that will make you pee in your bed. Raids in Yemen, killing ISIS, rounding up immigrants, provoking N. Korea, making up with N. Korea, raising tariffs, squashing the opposition - and *if we're all lucky* - putting Hillary behind bars.

Huge applause followed by chants of: "Lock her up!"

DONALD J. TRUMP

When they first booked me for this HBO special, they said, President Trump, they said, what will your show be about? Will you talk about your policies, foreign and domestic, your doubts and fears? Or is it going to be more personal? *Funnier...?* Hold on I told them. Hold on! Wait! I never have any idea what I'll say or do until I do it. Keeps things more interesting.

He looks up to back of House.

DONALD J. TRUMP

Hey, can we do something with the lights here. Terrible. Terrible. I need a brighter spotlight. On me. Brighter halo on The Donald, thank you.

TRANSPARENT FALSEHOOD

Lights adjust.

                DONALD J. TRUMP
That's it. Better. Brighter. More *truthful!*
          (to Audience)
This show I told the folks at HBO, good folks, I know some of them a long time and I like them. Not everyone there is Bill Maher. And I told them, this show will make you laugh, cry, nothing like it. This show is for winners! And look at you. Here. The lucky ones to have gotten seats, not everyone can be that lucky. Hottest ticket in town. You should see how many people we had to turn away. So many. So sad. But what are you going to do? When you're this popular it's not easy. Some of them I'm sorry to say are at *Hamilton* now. Second rate show, lots of hype. Shit hole theater! SHIT HOLE! Not nearly as good. Not like this. You guys are the lucky ones.
          (Sips water.)
Wow! I look at you guys and I almost envy you. Yes I do. Scoring the hottest ticket in town. I mean who's dick did you suck or *pussy you grab* (pardon my French) to get a ticket for my amazing show? Who…? Because this limited HBO special, it's tough. No president has ever done this before. This isn't *HAMILTON*. I'm not doing some *fake history* in Black Face. But you guys already know that, don't you. You're smart. I can see that. Very savvy crowd we have here tonight.
          (Shouting into back of theater)
Can we get a shot of this amazing audience please!!
          (No answer)
I SAID… Nah, forget it. I'll have my own Crew do it.
          (to invisible Crew)

Ok, guys, you know what to do. I want a mixed demographic. Lots of black faces, the darker the better, and a few Hispanic folk. Seriously... you guys are a great house. Terrific. I can always tell a great house. Sometimes they are not so good... but you guys tonight... Great. The best. Go ahead. Clap for yourselves. You deserve it. You're all winners. Each and everyone of you.

Quick! Show of hands. How many here attended my inauguration. NO! Don't raise your hands. I'm sure you were all there - otherwise you wouldn't be here tonight. Boy, that was some day, wasn't it? A beautiful bookmark in the history of our great country. On its way to becoming even greater. And the crowds... so *huuuge*. People were watching this all over the world. All over. I even got a call from Queen Elizabeth crying. Sobbing. Wishing her own coronation could have been as popular and beautiful. Nobody's ever had an inauguration like this. Nobody. And she called me up, crying, the Queen, she called me to say. It was *gorgeous Donald. Absolutely gorgeous. I remain speechless.* Now let me tell you something you probably didn't know, and I probably shouldn't even be saying this, but the Queen, even at her age, started menstruating again she got so excited watching my inauguration. At her age. Royal blood. Had to be rushed to the hospital, but it was worth it she said. *Donald, it made me feel young again.* A fresh start. And that's what this country needs. A new beginning. With a little blood if necessary.
 (He suddenly singles out someone in the House.)
YOU! Over there. What are you writing? Oh, you're a critic. Really...? Most critics are professional liars. Read us what you're writing. Go ahead. I'm listening. How's it going so far?
 (Trump motions with thumb)

TRANSPARENT FALSEHOOD

Up? Down...? Good, bad? Because if it's down we know you're lying. A dishonest critic hired by the Opposition to pan me. Won't be the first time. But it won't work. Not tonight.

Someone in Audience begins to cough. Trump stops, focuses on cough.

Really...? Where is that? Who is that?

More coughing.

Who let this traitor in?

Another muffled cough.

I could have you shot you know and nothing would happen. Right where you're sitting. In the gallery. Like Lincoln. We need a sanctuary theater that's safe. Protected. *Thespian Lives Matter!*
(to Critic)
I hope you're getting all that.

A Tweet comes in on Trump's phone. He stops to read it.

DONALD J. TRUMP
What do you know. Wow, can't believe it. Should I share it with you? My latest tweet...? Sure. Why not. I just got a tweet from head of HBO. Good friend of mine. Smart guy. And guess what? They want me to extend the run of this show.
(to Critic)
See? Doesn't matter what garbage you're scribbling over there. Nobody cares.

(to an Audience member sitting next to Critic)
Can you look over his shoulder? See what he's writing. Ah, don't bother, I bet I already know. Their lies are so predictable. Unimaginative. *(as if reading)* "Witnessing President Trump's HBO special last night was not much different from watching a large orange Thanksgiving float work its way down 5th Avenue. With his great penchant for hyperbole and plenty of hot air, there was little substance to speak of."

See? That's what I've been saying all along. These folks, these *cosmopolitan elites* like using big words so they can feel important and better than you. *Penchant. Hyperbole.* Please! Why not just call it 'truthful exaggeration'. Works for me. But the Opposition will do anything to ruin my show. And that's why we need walls to *segregate* - God I love that word! - *segregate* us from them.
(He sips some water.)
The other day I had my annual check up. Amazing. Blood pressure, cholesterol levels, testosterone, simply amazing results. Actually… testosterone was high through the roof for someone my age. But I don't want to brag. Doctor had to clean his glasses to read my labs they were so good.

Donny, he said - we go way back, Dr Levy and me. Great Doctor. The best. Real mensch. *Is this for real, Donny?* He asked, staring at my testosterone. *You seem to be getting younger every year. Please promise me you'll donate your body to science. We need to see how you do it. How the fuck do you do it? Donny, that's the best Colon I've ever seen in my whole career… clean… beautiful, scented, I shit you not, not even the shadow of a polyp."*

Then he asks if he could use my colonoscopy footage for his medical class at Harvard. *Go ahead,* I said, *if it will help mankind, go ahead. Here look for yourself.*
　　　　　　(to back of Theater House)
Can you throw the footage up please. Should be all cued up.

Trump's colonoscopy footage plays on an upstage screen.

It's like a Disneyland ride in there, *Pirates of the Caribbean* meets *Toad's Wild Ride*. Pretty great, huh. Actually I stayed awake for mine. All the twists and turns. Stray bit of cashews from the night before. My colon is like a great dividing wall that keeps all the waste in one area so the rest of the body can stay clean and pure. And that's as close to metaphor as The Donald will ever get. So enjoy it. What do you all think? How are you enjoying the show so far? *(to Critic)* Not you! Not you!! But the rest of you… how's it going so far? Pretty good, huh. I can tell. Great show. I can always tell. Trump knows. The American people don't need more swamp lies.. They need something real now. Authentic. *American!* They need answers. No more lies! *(He begins to chant.)* No more lies! No more lies! No more lies!

Audience joins in. After a moment he raises his hand for silence.

DONALD J. TRUMP
My words tonight will cancel out all the lies that have built up and clotted your lives and soon the whole room will grow brighter as I talk and fill it with my words.
　　　　(As counterpoint - Lights Begin to Dim)
A new world order is coming. And it brings with it a new

kind of light. Truthful and blinding. A beautiful light you've never seen before. Honest and bright. Full of American pride and liberty. There are no borders in the dark, but that's also why we keep bumping into things... hurting ourselves... because of this darkness. And I won't allow that any longer. Not in my America. Which is why the *LIGHT* I'm bringing is so important.

Theater house gets progressively DARKER.

DONALD J. TRUMP
Room bright with a new kind of truth. My Truth! Nothing out there like it.

House Lights continue to Dim - as he talks about this new stunning Light.

I promise you it's the change we've all been waiting for. Trump's blinding eclipse. It's what you all need. Each and everyone of you. The light! So bright. Celestial and epic. Blinding unapologetic light!

Theater is almost completely dark by now. Lights out, the gas lighting complete.

(POSSIBLE INTERMISSION HERE)

4

AS YOUR BOSS AND BELOVED PRESIDENT

<u>Scene:</u> *Intermission. Trump and Bannon stand at a urinal. Side by side. Trump fumbles with small hands to remove his penis from his trousers.*

                BANNON
Is the second act shorter?

              DONALD J. TRUMP
Depends on how I feel.

              BANNON
Don't you have a script?

              DONALD J. TRUMP
A what…?

BANNON
What are you going to talk about *after* this intermission?

DONALD J. TRUMP
After intermission?

BANNON
Yeah.

DONALD J. TRUMP
Same shit as before. Tell 'em whatever they want to hear. Whatever I *think* they should hear.

BANNON
Good. So I won't be missing anything.

DONALD J. TRUMP
You're not staying…?

BANNON
I've got to take care of those… *leaks*. Remember?

DONALD J. TRUMP
Yes. Bad. Very bad. We need is to isolate those leaks and stop them from spreading. Bad people. Sick.

BANNON
It's those corporatist global forces.

DONALD J. TRUMP
Whatever. We need to stop those leaks pronto.

BANNON
Don't worry sir. We'll punish those responsible and put a finger in the damn of falsehood.

Trump fumbles to extricate his penis from his zipper and trousers.

DONALD J. TRUMP
Jesus, Steve, if I don't get this out fast I'll pee in my pants.
(*Trump finally finds his dick. Whips it out.*)
Ah! Got it! Little rascal.

He starts to pee as Intermission Lights Flicker.

DONALD J. TRUMP
Steve… you see the line to the women's room? If I had to wait that long I'd explode.

BANNON
They're lucky they don't have a prostate, sir.

DONALD J. TRUMP
As long as they can find mine, I don't care. Haha. That was a joke Steve.

BANNON (*fake laughs*)
Funny, sir.

DONALD J. TRUMP
Steve.

BANNON
Sir?

DONALD J. TRUMP
Take it out.

BANNON
What?

DONALD J. TRUMP
You heard me. Take out your pecker.

BANNON
I thought we are here to discuss the leaks.

DONALD J. TRUMP
We are. Now as your boss and beloved President I order you to take it out.

BANNON
What about the show?

Lights still flickering.

DONALD J. TRUMP
Trust me. No one's starting without me.

BANNON
But—

DONALD J.TRUMP
Just take it out.

BANNON
I just finished peeing.

DONALD J. TRUMP
I'm *not* going to pee alone. Take it out. You were in the Navy.

BANNON
What's that supposed to mean?

DONALD J. TRUMP
You peed around other men before.

BANNON *(hesitant)*
When I had to. Yes.

DONALD J. TRUMP
Maybe I should've given Governor Christie your job, eh? He'd be peeing with one hand, eating meatloaf with the other.

BANNON
You want to fire me, go ahead.

DONALD J. TRUMP
Relax. Nobody's firing anyone. *Yet.*

BANNON *(overlapping)*
Really? Because there've been leaks, you know. People have been talking about my so-called "resignation".

DONALD
People will say anything to cause trouble. Look at that Comey character... has to go and make a big fuss over nothing. For once I decide to show a little interest, for once, so I ask: *How's the job, Mr Comey? You like your job?* And next thing you know I'm obstructing justice.

BANNON
James Comey is a boy pussy who can't even suck his own cock.

DONALD J. TRUMP
It wasn't a threat. I just—

BANNON
Of course not. No.

DONALD J. TRUMP
I just ask everyone that question.

BANNON
Always thinking of others.

DONALD J. TRUMP
Exactly.

BANNON
An altruistic show of concern mixed with a bit of executive privilege.

DONALD J. TRUMP
So. You like working for me, Steve?

BANNON
I'll go to war for you, sir. You know that.

DONALD J. TRUMP
Great. Then take out you pecker.

Bannon hesitates.

DONALD J. TRUMP
Go on. You don't except me to help you.

BANNON
I don't need your help.

DONALD J. TRUMP
How can I expect you to take a bullet for me Steve if you won't even touch your own dick when I ask you to?

BANNON
Ok, ok, I got it. I've got it.

Bannon reluctantly takes out his dick, although he doesn't have to pee. Trump looks over, then takes a pic of it on his phone. Tweets.

BANNON
What did you just tweet?

DONALD J. TRUMP
A picture.

                    BANNON
Of what?

                    DONALD J. TRUMP
Check your phone.

BING! He does.

                    BANNON *(reading Tweet on phone)*
Always bigger@realDonaldJTrump
                    (Puts phone down.)
Really…?

                    DONALD J. TRUMP
What?

                    BANNON
So puerile.

                    DONALD J. TRUMP
What's that…?

                    BANNON
You switched the pictures.

                    DONALD J. TRUMP
No I didn't.

                    BANNON
You flipped them around. That's *my* dick under *your* name.

DONALD J. TRUMP
Next you're going to tell me that Obama had a larger inauguration and those Park images were also... *flipped*.

BANNON
You can' let anything go, can you?

DONALD J. TRUMP
Sure I can. *(changing topic, peering over)* You circumcised, Steve?

BANNON
With all due respect, sir. None of your business.

DONALD J. TRUMP
Ooo. Touchy. They say you don't like Jews. Is that true?

BANNON
In general no. But there are exceptions.

DONALD J. TRUMP
You know my daughter is Jewish. *Now.*

BANNON
I was sorry to hear that, sir.

DONALD J. TRUMP
Actually converted. But so far it's been good. Helpful with the electoral demographic.

BANNON
She can always convert back.

DONALD J. TRUMP
It's not like Halloween. You don't just put it on and take it off.

BANNON
I've always maintained the Inquisition needed better tools.

Trump regards him, puzzled.

Lights Flicker accompanied by a peremptory Intermission Bell.

DONALD J. TRUMP
So what are we doing about these leaks? Bad for moral. Security. It has to stop. I want those people crucified. We need to set an example.

BANNON
I told you. I'm all over it.

DONALD J. TRUMP
Good. And while you're at it, I want tonight's critic investigated. Have a bad feeling about that one. Way he was *writing* things down.

BANNON
Probably Jewish.

DONALD J. TRUMP
Where's the FBI or CIA when you need them?

BANNON
I think you've alienated them both, sir, when you compared them to Nazis.

DONALD J. TRUMP
A little criticism is good for you. Makes you work harder. Look at me.

BANNON
Maybe you shouldn't tweet so much.

DONALD J. TRUMP
You still sore about your *dick pic.* Is that it…?

BANNON
No. But you should—

DONALD J. TRUMP *(overlapping)*
What?! I should WHAT?! Are you suggesting I'm the source of the leaks? Your own *President and Commander-in-Chief.*

BANNON
Of course not. But that *is* an old unsecured phone sir. And—

DONALD J. TRUMP *(cutting him off)*
Deal with it! My phone is <u>MY</u> phone. Have you looked at Hillary's server? I'll use whatever fucking phone I want!!

BANNON
But Hillary's not President sir - you are.

                    DONALD J. TRUMP
Don't start me with her.

                         BANNON
I didn't. You did.

                    DONALD J. TRUMP
That blood-letting witch cooking kids up in her pizza store. Talk about witch hunt. They should burn her at the stake. Having all those dead immigrants coming out of their grave to vote for a nasty woman like that . Please. It's disgraceful. Sick. Un-American. We need to deal with this the old Russian way. Just make the troubles go away.

                         BANNON
You're not suggesting.

                    DONALD J. TRUMP
Russians "*disappear*" people all the time.

                         BANNON
I guess they're more *evolved* than we are in this respect.

                    DONALD J. TRUMP
Or North Korea. Even better. You know that Little Rocket Man uses artillery shells to get rid of his opposition? Like they were never even *born*. Very talented guy.

                   BANNON *(whispering)*
You really shouldn't be saying these things, sir.

DONALD J. TRUMP
Why are you whispering?

BANNON
What if someone's listening now.

DONALD J. TRUMP
More leaks…? *Here!?*

BANNON
Possible. It's always possible. For all we know, Obama might have left us a few presents.

DONALD J. TRUMP
(turns to toilet stalls, sniffs)
I don't smell anything.

BANNON
I didn't mean that, sir.
(whispering)
I wouldn't be surprised if those cakes in the urinals were in fact listening devices.

DONALD J. TRUMP
You think?

BANNON
No way of knowing.

DONALD J. TRUMP
Pick it up and check.

BANNON

I....

DONALD J. TRUMP

Do it!

Bannon reluctantly obliges and picks up a urinal cake to inspect it. Grimaces with disgust as it drips urine in his hand.

DONALD J. TRUMP

Now put it to your ear.

BANNON

No.

DONALD J. TRUMP

I thought you said you heard something.

BANNON

I'm not doing this.

DONALD J. TRUMP

Steve! Do I need to call Jared…?

Bannon obliges and listens to the dripping urinal cake. Then drops it back in the urinal. Goes to wash his hands and face.

DONALD J. TRUMP

Well…?

                          BANNON
Nothing. But it still feels like we're being spied on.

                       DONALD J. TRUMP
We are.

                          BANNON
What?

                       DONALD J. TRUMP
Being *observed*. Not spied. Big difference.

                          BANNON
Wha—

                       DONALD J. TRUMP
But don't worry. It's only my crew. Not real spies.

                          BANNON
Crew…?

                       DONALD J. TRUMP
The one you recommended. Don't you remember?

                          BANNON
I don't recall ever—

                       DONALD J. TRUMP
Hiding like Ninja. Day or night. Amazing bunch. Terrific!

                          BANNON
I don't see anyone.

DONALD J. TRUMP

At first I wanted to hire a National Geographic team. Those guys are good. The best. The way they can film animals in their habitat. You ever see those shows? Amazing. How they capture those animals without them knowing it. All natural. Nothing phony. *FAKE*. Whales having sex in the ocean deep. Amazing stuff. Because it's real. The size of those things. Their penises. You have to respect that. *Yuuuge.* But you told me not to. You talked me out of it.

Bannon dries his hands.

BANNON

I did…?

DONALD J. TRUMP

I have just the perfect crew for you, you said. *You'll need a crew that's good with people,* you said. *Humans not Animals.*

But what - I asked you - *what about all those animals catching and eating all the other animals. All those winners feeding on all those losers? You gotta love it.*

No! - you shouted, turning all red in the face, your nose - *Donald J. Trump will not be anthropomorphized… no matter what, he will not be anthropomorphized!*

I looked up that word and you were right. So I went with the film crew you recommended and they're incredible. I love these guys. The best. Catching me at *my* best. Together we'll set the record straight once and for all.

Light flicker more urgently.

BANNON
I really think it's time you return to the show, sir.

DONALD J. TRUMP
You let me worry about that. *(Beat)* You ever see *Braveheart*, Steve?

BANNON
Years ago. Why? Should I see it again?

DONALD J. TRUMP
Nah. Just gets you thinking about betrayal… these leaks. The people who sold Mel Gibson out.
   (clear his throat, quotes grandly from opening of
       Braveheart)
"Historians will tell you I'm a liar, but history was written by those who hung heroes."

BANNON
I saw *Mad Max* recently. Very inspirational. It was on tv in the background while I was crafting your executive order.

DONALD J. TRUMP
Still holds up I bet.

BANNON
More relevant than ever. They had this *Mad Max* marathon on AMC. A world of such deconstructed chaos. Invention. *Tribal isolationism.* I really loved it.

So much to learn from it. Most people live from one snooze slap on the alarm to the next… what I want is to really shake things up!!

DONALD J. TRUMP
Ugh, please, Steve, you always bore the shit out of me with that global stuff.

BANNON
It's important to have a vision, sir.

DONALD J. TRUMP *(insinuating)*
Save it for your… *interviews.*

BANNON
I… I've been meaning to talk to you about that, sir.

DONALD J. TRUMP
Think I wouldn't see them just because I don't read?

BANNON
Of course not, sir.

DONALD J. TRUMP
Trump's Brain. Is that what we call ourselves now?

BANNON
You know the press, sir, the way they lie and twist everything.

DONALD J. TRUMP
Truth is there'd be *No Bannon Without Trump.* And that's no alternate fact.

BANNON
Absolutely agree, sir.

DONALD J. TRUMP
Good. Then find me those leaks. A lot of suspicious faces working on the Hill and in the White House if you ask me.

BANNON *(under his breath)*
Jews.

DONALD J. TRUMP
What's that?

BANNON
A lot of Jews roaming about in those halls.

DONALD J. TRUMP
Tell me the truth Steve, and I'm not going to hold it against you, but what's your problem with Jews? I've always found them very good in business… especially that Roy Cohn.

BANNON
They serve a purpose, sir.

DONALD J. TRUMP
And what do you think of Jared? He's pretty sharp. You gotta give him that. Even Henry Kissinger says Jared is the next Henry Kissenger.

BANNON
KISS-enger can *KISS* my ass.

DONALD J. TRUMP
You think he's wrong?

BANNON
I think Ivanka could've done better.

DONALD J. TRUMP
Me too!! Me too!! But I was already married. hahaha. She's hot, isn't she, my little Ivanka?

BANNON
She is sir. Even as a nouveau Jewess convert she holds much appeal. Which reminds me: *What's worse than Rosie O'Donnell?*

DONALD J. TRUMP
Nothing. Nothing's worse than Rosie O'Donnell!

BANNON
Rosie O'Donnell *converting* to Judaism.

DONALD J. TRUMP
Not funny. *Almost* funny. But too scary to be funny.
(They laugh.)
Didn't you make your money on *Seinfeld*, Steve?

BANNON
Purely speculative. I was young. Made my money. Got out.

DONALD J. TRUMP
I bet you did alright.

BANNON
Now I'm shaping policy… doing much more *important* things.

DONALD J. TRUMP
Good. I'm glad. Making people laugh is overrated. Especially when you can make them cry. Did you revise the latest Musl- *(hasitly corrects himself)*… immigration ban?

BANNON
Almost there. Just need to make it a bit more vague.

DONALD J. TRUMP
Is that what we want? *More* vague…?

BANNON
The vaguer the better. Leaves it wide open to interpretation. And the more ways we can interpret something, the more power it gives us.

DONALD J. TRUMP
Smart.

BANNON *(under his breath)*
Smarter than Jared.

DONALD J. TRUMP
What's that…?

BANNON
I said you'd be amazed at some of the things I've got lined up for us, sir. Things that you or I could never dream of. Things that could never be undone.

DONALD J. TRUMP
No. *About Jared.* You said something…

BANNON
I don't want to poison the well but…

DONALD J. TRUMP *(urinating)*
Go on. I've still got a few drops left. Your job is safe with me.

BANNON
These Jews. Always think they're the funniest and smartest in the room.

DONALD J. TRUMP
You've got to admit. They may not be the greatest golfers, but they've done alright for themselves.

BANNON *(shrugs)*
Maybe. But their petty intelligence and usury won't work in my new world order. Who wants to live in a world where you're always complaining and kvetching about the small insignificant things. We need to embrace the crisis and think BIG. That's why I never found *Seinfeld* very funny.

DONALD J. TRUMP
I'll be honest Steve, I kind of liked that show. That Julia Louis Dreyfuss is kind of hot.

BANNON
Always aggrieved about something. These Jews. Always wronged. These... *cosmopolitans*. Have you noticed that? Always asking you to apologize for something. Like you knocked over their gravestone or something.

DONALD J. TRUMP
And that's why I'm sending Pence instead of you to visit the Nazi death camps on his next trip to Europe. Unless you really want to go?

BANNON
Absolutely not, sir. Wouldn't catch me dead there. No pun intended.

DONALD J. TRUMP
You're not a Holocaust denier too, are you Steve?

BANNON
Some bad shit happened to some nameless people. Let's just leave it at that.

DONALD J. TRUMP
Ok, but you still have to tell Pence he needs to cry when he's there in front of that pile of shoes... mountain of hair. Terrible stuff. Almost can't believe it really happened.

BANNON *(doubtful)*
The whole thing is a bit much, isn't it…?

DONALD J. TRUMP
Fake…?

BANNON
All kinds of stories. Rumors.

DONALD J. TRUMP
I'll say. How many Jews did Schindler save… in that movie?

BANNON
They say… around 1200.

DONALD J. TRUMP
I could have tripled that on a bad day. Nobody's as good a deal maker as Donald J. Trump. Not even Oskar Schindler! *(He stares at his own dick.)* Help me shake the last drops.

BANNON
Sir…?

DONALD J. TRUMP
Just kidding. No man touches my dick except me.

Intermission Lights Pulse furiously - as he fumbles to get his dick back in his pants.

DONALD J. TRUMP
Come. My audience is waiting.

5

AS YOUR GOYISHE DADDY AND PRESIDENT

<u>Scene:</u> *Passover Seder at Mar-a-Lago. Just Trump and Ivanka and Jared. Their kids are running offstage, shouting, looking for the hidden Matzoh known as 'Afikomen'.*

The seder table is enormous. Too large. They have to shout across to be heard.

JARED *(shouting)*
How did Eric and Don Jr. get by in China?

DONALD J. TRUMP
Pretty good. Pretty good. We've been granted another 12 licensing brands. One of them for an *escort* service.

JARED
Aren't you worried about emoluments?

DONALD J. TRUMP
Got to make sure Melania has work once we leave the White House.

IVANKA
Dad!

DONALD J. TRUMP
Just kidding. This wine! I never drink, but tonight you said is supposed to be different. So I'm having a little drink.

IVANKA
Be careful you don't overdo it, daddy.

He empties glass.

DONALD J. TRUMP
Look Jared. Most Americans can't even pronounce the word - *emolument* - let alone know what it means. Which is great for me. People just want to be left alone. That's why they have government. Everyone's too busy living the chaos of their little lives. Struggling from one crazy moment to the next. Besides, relax, you guys are all gonna get Ethics Waivers.

JARED
That might not be enough. Given the scope of…

IVANKA *(overlapping)*
Please, honey. Don't argue with Daddy. Daddy is going to get a Nobel prize for what he did with North Korea.

DONALD J. TRUMP
Not just any Nobel Prize, babe, but Obama's personal one. They're gonna take back the one they gave him - and give it to me.

JARED
Can they do that?

IVANKA
Jared!

JARED
What? I just -

IVANKA *(overlapping)*
"Those who say it can not be done, should not interrupt those doing it."

JARED
Wasn't that in your fortune cookie last night?

IVANKA
Please! I'm just so glad we're having seder at Mar-a-Lago, daddy. Thank you.

She leans over to give Trump a kiss. Long, uncomfortable. Jared coughs. They look up.

JARED *(shouting)*
This table is so big.

DONALD J. TRUMP
I know. I thought more people would show.

IVANKA
Who else did you invite?

DONALD J. TRUMP
Melania… Barron… but he has too much school work these days. Your two brothers, but they are busy expanding the brand, *not Tiffany*, and Steve of course.

JARED *(disgusted)*
Miller…? Doesn't he have his own seder to go to?

DONALD J. TRUMP
No. *Bannon*. He said he'd try to make it but wasn't sure.

Ivanka and Jared share a concerned look.

DONALD J. TRUMP
Relax… just kidding. I fired his sloppy ass ages ago.

IVANKA
You know Daddy, a lot of people say he might have been the source behind all those leaks.

DONALD J. TRUMP
Fuck Bannon and his small conspiracy dick!
(He gets up and begins to move place settings around.)
Come on. Let's get closer together. I'm tired of shouting across this table like Charles Foster Kane screaming at Susan Alexander.

IVANKA

Who's she?

DONALD J. TRUMP

Citizen Kane. You must have seen it. Not as good as *Braveheart* but some movie. The emptiness he feels. The betrayal.

(With relish) Rosebud.

He lets the word hang. Long protracted silence, interminable, as he stares into space.

IVANKA

Dad...?

DONALD J. TRUMP *(snapping back)*

Rosebud. So much damage from one word. So sad. And that scene where they are alone at dinner, sitting across from each other at the longest table in history, shouting into the void. The *void.*

JARED

Be careful with the seder plate.

DONALD J. TRUMP

I've got it.

They finish rearranging table. Sit.

DONALD J. TRUMP

So now let me get it straight there are usually two dinners.

JARED
Yes.

DONALD J. TRUMP
On consecutive nights.

JARED
Yes.

DONALD J. TRUMP
So one of these days is an *"alternate seder night"*.

JARED
Not exactly... *alternate*.

DONALD J. TRUMP
A *fake* Passover.

JARED
No, no. I didn't say that.

IVANKA
That's not how it works, Daddy.

JARED
They are both meant to be real. And of *equal* importance.

DONALD J. TRUMP
So which are we doing tonight?

IVANKA
Does it matter...?

DONALD J. TRUMP
I just hope it's the one that's more real of the two. After all I am not only your *goyishe* Daddy but also your President.

IVANKA
Your Yiddish is getting pretty good, Daddy, isn't it Jared?

JARED
Sure is.
(Kids shouting offstage.)
I better go check on the kids. Been a while.

IVANKA
They still looking for the *afikomen*...?

DONALD J. TRUMP
When Trump hides money it stays hidden. Offshore accounts or Passover matzoh, it's the same to me.

JARED
I'll be right back.

Jared exits to check up on kids. Trump and Ivanka alone. Pause.

DONALD J. TRUMP
You're looking good, babe.

IVANKA
Thanks, daddy.

DONALD J. TRUMP
Motherhood suits you.

IVANKA
You think…?

DONALD J. TRUMP
You still have your figure.

IVANKA
It's important for the business.

DONALD J. TRUMP
A lot of these young women today think they have license to just let themselves go because they're mothers now. *Your* mother… Ivana… great mother! Took care of everything… *as well as her figure.* You kids were lucky that way.

IVANKA
I just wish we had seder as kids. Seems like so much fun.

DONALD J. TRUMP
You had Easter! Much better. BIGGER!

IVANKA
Did you have a good childhood, daddy?

DONALD J. TRUMP *(muttering to self)*
Childhood…?

Another long labyrinthine silence, almost haunting.

                    IVANKA
Daddy… are you ok?

                  DONALD J. TRUMP
What?

                 IVANKA *(overlap)*
I asked about your childhood… if it was…

              DONALD J. TRUMP *(overlap)*
Fine, I guess. I spent all of mine waiting to grow up and be famous.

            IVANKA *(striving to cheer him up)*
Remember that time we played Monopoly? I must've been around 15. You never liked playing board games but you agreed to play because I just broke up with Jimmy Barbino and I wouldn't stop crying…

                  DONALD J. TRUMP
I hated all your boyfriends. But this guy….what a loser, I bet he's in jail doing hard time now…

              IVANKA *(suddenly souring)*
But even then you couldn't let me win. No.

                  DONALD J. TRUMP
I tried. I swear to you I tried. It's just not in me. To lose and let others win. Not even my own kids.

                    IVANKA
And when I was so down and heartbroken you made me

sell you all my properties so you could bankrupt me. Your *own* daughter.

DONALD J. TRUMP

No point in playing if you're not going to win.

IVANKA

Years later Don Jr. told me you cheated and stole money from the Monopoly Bank when no one was looking.

DONALD J. TRUMP

Your fault for letting me be banker.

IVANKA

Is that what you told your Taj Mahal stock holders?

DONALD J. TRUMP *(sharp)*

Watch it, hon.

IVANKA

Relax Dad. I'm supposed to be a moderating influence on you.

DONALD J. TRUMP

Is that so…?

IVANKA

I've been reading Eleanor Roosevelt's biography and she said: *The most important thing in any relationship is not what you get, but what you give.*

                    DONALD J. TRUMP
Loser.

                         IVANKA
Dad!

          DONALD J. TRUMP *(empties wine)*
I had a *STORMY* dream about you the other night, hon.

                         IVANKA
Again?

                    DONALD J. TRUMP
This was different, it was *you* but it wasn't *you*. Know what I mean? And in this *stormy* dream you made me sign a non-disclosure so that even if I remembered what happened when I woke up - I couldn't talk about it.

                         IVANKA
Did you…?

                    DONALD J. TRUMP
What…?

                         IVANKA
Remember it?

                    DONALD J. TRUMP
What do you think…?

A charged moment between Father and daughter. Jared enters.

IVANKA

Kids okay…?

JARED

They're still searching. All excited.

DONALD J. TRUMP

Maybe we should start this seder thing without them.
    (He empties his wine glass.)
I never drink. Never. But you're right, tonight is different from all other nights.
    (He empties another glass.)
And you Jared are not only going to bring peace to that camel infested patch of sand in the Middle east, but I also want you to discover the secret to immortality!

Trump reaches for another full glass at the center of the table. Jared stops him.

JARED

No, NO!

DONALD J. TRUMP *(misconstruing)*

What's wrong, Jared? Am I asking too much of you? Is that too tall an order?

JARED

No. That glass. In your hand. It's not for drinking.

DONALD J. TRUMP

Poisoned? Haha.

JARED
It's for the Elijah the Prophet and the heralding of the Messiah.

DONALD J. TRUMP *(abstracted, haunted)*
The Messiah... really?

JARED
Tonight we leave the front door open, inviting him to come in and have a glass of wine.

DONALD J. TRUMP
I just hope he can get past the secret service.

JARED
I don't think that's a problem for the Messiah.

DONALD J. TRUMP
Maybe not, ok, but will he sign a film release?

JARED
What...?

IVANKA
Dad's doing this project, hon. *(to Trump)* You haven't told him?

DONALD J. TRUMP
I've hired a crew to tape me 24/7.

JARED
Are they here now?

DONALD J. TRUMP
Like Ninja. No one can see them they're so good.

JARED *(overlapping)*
On *yom tov!?* They have to leave.

DONALD J. TRUMP
I'll make you a deal.

JARED
This is an important holiday. No deals, especially from the *Shabbat Goy.*

DONALD J. TRUMP
Think of all the good it would do the Jews to show footage of the President having seder dinner at his Mar-a-Lago home.

IVANKA *(to Jared)*
He's right, hon. Daddy is always right.

Jared relents. Trump makes a toast with the Messiah glass.

DONALD J. TRUMP
To the Messiah and the end of times! *(He empties the Messiah glass himself.)* To me! And Rosebud!

6

AS CLASSROOM GUEST
AND YOUR PRESIDENT

<u>Scene:</u> *Trump visits Barron's Classroom. He tosses "Make America Great" caps to the students. He is flanked by two burly Secret Service guys who are dressed as Professional Wrestlers. Next to them is the Teacher.*

TEACHER
Class! Class! I can understand how excited you all are with your new hats. But please let's settle down for our very special parents day guest. Let's give a warm welcome to Barron's father - and our 45th President - Donald J. Trump - who took time out of his very busy schedule to come here and visit with us today.

Applause. Trump smiles and soaks it in. Motions for more applause.

TEACHER
Now I hope President Trump won't mind leading us in the Pledge of Allegiance before we begin.

DONALD J. TRUMP
Of course. Anything for our great country.

TEACHER
Everyone please stand. And please remove your Make America Great hats.

Class stands. Trumps launches into his version of the Pledge Allegiance. A thin echo of Students join him.

DONALD J. TRUMP
I pledge allegiance to the amazing flag of the United States of America, which I President Donald J. Trump made great again. And to the Republic-an Agenda for which it now stands. One Nation... One Nation...
  (*He seems to forget his lines, one of the Secret Service Wrestlers whispers in his ear.*)
One Nation.... under God, indivisible, with liberty and justice for all - except illegal immigrants and those who wish us harm. America first!!
  (*He gives a Sieg Heil salute*)
Amen!

TEACHER (*tears in her eyes*)
That was so beautiful. So moving. Thank you.

Trump offers a phony smile.

TEACHER
President Trump will now give you a brief glimpse of what the job of being president for the most powerful country in the world entails.

DONALD J. TRUMP
Thank you Miss....

TEACHER *(filling in)*
Esposito.

DONALD J. TRUMP *(double-take)*
Where were you born Miss.... *Esposito?*

TEACHER
In New Mexico.

DONALD J. TRUMP
Sure it wasn't *old* Mexico?

TEACHER
No sir. Born and bred right here in the United States. We were never allowed to speak a word of Spanish outside the home or in public, and always used sunscreen while doing gardening jobs so our skin won't darken too much.

DONALD J. TRUMP
See, class! That's the kind of immigrant our country needs.

TEACHER
Thank you President Trump.

DONALD J. TRUMP
You're welcome Miss Enchilada.
(looking her over)
You by any chance carrying…?

TEACHER
You could tell? Really?
(proudly massaging belly)
Am I already showing…?

DONALD J. TRUMP
I meant your class rifle… these kids need protection. This isn't the America I grew up in. A glorious America which we carelessly lost, and which as your President, is my job to find again.
(He snorts.)
When I was a kid things were so much different then. Much more… civilized. Back then you needed permission to go to the bathroom. A "hall pass". And you went to the bathroom of your assigned sex. None of this liberal hanky panky going on. Then when you got home you ate hot apple pie before going out to play stickball. Later, when your folks were watching *un-fake* news in the other room, you'd steal a look at your dad's torn Playboy featuring fake breasts before going to bed. If you were a girl, you'd be mending socks or knitting a sweater with needles that were *never* to be used for any other purpose than knitting. That was the kind of America I grew up in. And the kind of America I'm wrestling hard now to win back for you as your freely elected President.

But how, you may ask, will The Donald achieve this? What is he going to do? Good question. Smart class. You can find part of the answers in my new HBO show, which I hope you've all seen.

STUDENT #1
Past my bedtime.

STUDENT #2
Me too.

DONALD J. TRUMP
That's not good. Tell your mother I give you permission to watch it. Tell her it's now part of the curriculum. And you *must* watch it. Isn't that so, Miss Chile Relleno ?

TEACHER
Yes, Mr. President. It is now mandatory *and* required.

DONALD J. TRUMP
I know it airs late and isn't big on special effects, but I'm surprised at you kids. How do you expect to make a change if you don't know what's going on. Besides, it's captivating stuff. Finally a show for all ages that will also make you smarter. *(Beat)* Now are there any questions before we go forward?

Some kid raises their hand and stands. Trump squints his eyes angrily.

DONALD J. TRUMP
Not you. Not you!! Sit down. You are trouble.

STUDENT (TOMMY)
But -

DONALD J. TRUMP
Tommy, yes…? I've heard a lot about you. None of it good.

TOMMY
I didn't do anything.

DONALD J. TRUMP
You ratted out on my son on the math test.

TOMMY
But he was cheating.

DONALD J. TRUMP
Sit down. Sit down!

TOMMY
He was.

BARRON
No I wasn't.

DONALD J. TRUMP
How do we know you weren't cheating from him? *Cheater*!

TOMMY
I would never do that.

DONALD J. TRUMP

Hillary cheated. They gave her questions to the debate. And she said nothing. But believe me, stealing questions is worse than providing answers. And you know what we do with cheaters?

BARRON

Lock them up.

TOMMY

Wait a minute.

A chorus of students begin to chant. "Lock him up! Lock him up!" Trump motions to the security guard/wrestler to remove Tommy from class.

TOMMY

I didn't do anything!!!

DONALD J. TRUMP

Go on, Barron. *(He motions for Barron to join them.)* Make me proud Barron.

TOMMY

This isn't fair. I didn't do anything.

DONALD J. TRUMP

You brought this on yourself. You can't just rat someone out and expect the leaks to go unpunished.

As they drag Tommy out.

TOMMY
Please!! No!

DONALD J. TRUMP
Don't be a sissy Barron! Use the *Cold Steve Austin Stunner* on him.

TOMMY
I didn't do anything. Please!

As we hear Tommy being beaten offstage.

DONALD J. TRUMP
Now anyone here remember *Wrestelmania 23*. I know it's before any of you were born, but isn't that what Youtube is for?

STUDENT
Is that where you fight Vince McMahon and make him shave his head?

DONALD J. TRUMP
That's right. Smart kid. You get an A!

STUDENT#2
My dad says it was all fake. The wrestling. Just like you.

DONALD J. TRUMP
Really?

STUDENT#2
He says you're a fake president.

Turns to Teacher, sinister

              DONALD J. TRUMP
I need this boy's info and address.

Outside the beating stops and an Ambulance siren is heard.

              DONALD J. TRUMP
Ok. Show of hands: How many other parents talk about me at home? Good or bad things…. how many?

More hands go up.

              DONALD J. TRUMP
You. What do they say?

              STUDENT#3
My mom….

              DONALD J. TRUMP
Yes?

              STUDENT#3
…. she thinks you are still pretty hot at your age.

              DONALD J. TRUMP
Really…? How old is your mom?

              STUDENT#3
Thirty-five but she tells everyone it's thirty-two.

DONALD J. TRUMP *(to Teacher)*
I'll need this kid's home info and address as well. *(lascivious)* Tell your mom I send my regards.

Barron enters with Wrestlers/Secret Service, no sign of Tommy. Blood everywhere.

DONALD J. TRUMP
Where's your friend?

BARRON
I think I overdid it with the dropkicks and knee drops.

Ambulance in distance.

DONALD J. TRUMP
Better to go big than small. Unless you're bombing Syria. Then you want to go small, so you don't piss off Russia.

STUDENT
Can we play with the football now?

ANOTHER STUDENT
Yeah. Barron promised us you'd let us play with it.

DONALD J. TRUMP
Is that true Barron?

Barron lowers head.

BARRON
Yes.

DONALD J. TRUMP
The "Football" is a very serious thing. How many of you know what uranium is. What? No one doing a class report on uranium?

STUDENTS
-We want to play with the football.
-Yeah! Football!!
-Football yeah! Football yeah!!

DONALD J. TRUMP
Uranium is a very powerful thing that can be used for good things, but also for bad things. When you use it for bad things, like bombs, it can cause a lot of pain. A lot. Your eyes melt in your head and you can't breathe. Nobody wants that.

He motions to the Wrestlers to get the "football". They ceremoniously lay it on the Teacher' table.

DONALD J. TRUMP
What we really need is a military on viagra. A military with a hard-on and a crazy man willing to jerk it off at the trigger. *(He approaches the football. Caresses it.)* Who else will protect you, if not me? Who else?!

All at once a shrill piercing ALARM goes off. Unlike anything heard before.

DONALD J. TRUMP
What's that?! What's going on??? Did anyone touch it? Who the fuck touched the football?! ANY KID TOUCHING THE FOOTBALL WILL BE SHOT.

Secret Service Wrestlers quickly huddle and surround Trump.

              WRESTLER/SECRET SERVICE
It's North Korea sir. They just launched another ballistic missile.

              DONALD J. TRUMP
You sure it wasn't Canada…?

              WRESTLER/SECRET SERVICE
No, sir.

              DONALD J. TRUMP
But Kim Jong Un is an honorable dictator who gave me his word. Not like that weak Trudeau who'll stab you in the back without so much as the courtesy of a reach-around

              WRESTLER/SECRET SERVICE
Sir! What do you want us to do?

              DONALD J. TRUMP
We had a very special bond. Signed a very comprehensive agreement.

              WRESTLER/SECRET SERVICE
We need to do something.

              DONALD J. TRUMP
I can't believe he'd do this to me.

7

AS YOUR FAVORITE PATIENT AND PRESIDENT

<u>Scene:</u> *Doctor's Office. Trump is having a checkup. Doctor takes his blood pressure.*

DOCTOR
How are you doing Donald?

DONALD J. TRUMP
How am I doing? The Donald is doing great. Have no idea why I even made this appointment.

DOCTOR
Actually it was Congress, they insisted you come here.

DONALD J. TRUMP
That explains it. Because I feel great. Never felt better.

                  DOCTOR
What about all the stress?

                DONALD J. TRUMP
Press…?

                  DOCTOR
No I said *stress.*

                DONALD J. TRUMP
Never had more fun in my life.

                  DOCTOR
All that negative news? Must take its toll on you. No…?

                DONALD J. TRUMP
Negative press.   Vicious lies. I don't hear any of it anymore.

Trump smiles disingenuously. Long pause.

                  DOCTOR
Want to tell me about what happened in that classroom?

                DONALD J. TRUMP
Nothing happened.

                  DOCTOR
Your bodyguards got inappropriately physical with one of the other students.

> DONALD J. TRUMP

They just held him down while Barron dispensed some justice.

> DOCTOR

He ended up in the hospital.

> DONALD J. TRUMP

It's good to teach them discipline at a young age.

> DOCTOR

And the "football" ? Is it true what they say about you allowing kids to play with the "football"?

> DONALD J. TRUMP

Didn't you play football as a kid?

> DOCTOR

Donald. You know what I mean.

DOCTOR removes blood pressure band.

> DONALD J. TRUMP

How's the blood pressure?

> DOCTOR

110 over 80.

> DONALD J. TRUMP

Is that good?

DOCTOR
Like a teenager!

DONALD J. TRUMP
You know I still wake up with an erection every morning.

DOCTOR
That's very presidential.

DONALD J. TRUMP
Like raising the flag, I salute my erection every single morning.

He salutes his crotch.

DOCTOR
You are a great specimen, Donny. If I could only clone you the world would be a better place.

DONALD J. TRUMP
I smell a promotion coming.

DOCTOR
Thank you, sir. *(Beat)* How's the HBO show doing…?

DONALD J. TRUMP
They begged me to do another season. Nobody ever had a show like this. *Nobody!*
   (DOCTOR *listens to his chest.*)
You know the old saying…

DOCTOR
Cough.

Trump obliges. Coughs.

DONALD J. TRUMP
I think it was Confucius, or some other wise Oriental man, that said: *If you don't know how to juggle, just throw all your balls up in the air and run.*

DOCTOR
Your lungs seem fine. How's your sleep?

DONALD J. TRUMP
Sleep….? Can't make money if you're sleeping.

DOCTOR
No… you can't.

DONALD J. TRUMP
But I do have this recurring dream.

DOCTOR
I'm not a shrink, Donny. But go on.

DONALD J. TRUMP *(exploding)*
Think I'd be talking to a shrink?!

DOCTOR
It might —

TRANSPARENT FALSEHOOD

DONALD J. TRUMP *(overlap, upset)*
Believe me, there's nothing they want more than to throw Amendment 25 paragraph 4 at me. Think I don't know that? Fuck this new Congress! Ever since I got rid of their FBI poster boy they've been after me. My family. These stupid check ups,
(Trump suddenly drops his shorts and bends over.)
Go ahead. Shove your arthritic finger up my ass, I don't care. You can put your whole hand in. Hell. I'll even shove a finger up yours. As long as it gets me what I want and you give me a pair of gloves.

DOCTOR
I'd prefer if you just pulled up your pants and told me your dream, Donny.

He pulls up pants, fastens belt. Narrates dream.

DONALD J. TRUMP
Ok, ok. so I'm playing this game with my father. Great man my father. A real winner. And we're playing this game, you know. Where you rest your hands in another person's hands and they try to slap them before you can pull them away.
(Trump extends his open hands.)
Go ahead. Put your hands in mine, Doc. Rest them here. In the palm of my hands.

Doctor obliges.

                    DONALD J. TRUMP
Relax.

Doctor tries to smile. His hands resting, trembling on Trump's upturned palms.

                    DONALD J. TRUMP
So in this dream…

He slaps Doctor's hands, hard.

                    DONALD J. TRUMP
Don't let me distract you.
          (He extends his hands again for the DOCTOR.)
Again.

                    DOCTOR
I…

                    DONALD J. TRUMP
I can't have my doctor be a loser, can I…?

Doctor reluctantly returns his smarting hands on top of Trump's.

                    DONALD J. TRUMP
Although I'll have you know, I never lose at this. That's why I'm so good at deal making. My father taught me this. Before I was even toilet trained, he taught me how to play this game. Ruthless. Violent. Sometimes my hands would bleed for weeks.

> *(conspiratorial)*
>
> Between you and me, I think that's why my hands never got any bigger. Like the bound feet of those Japanese geishas.

Again Trump slaps at Doctor's hands.

> DONALD J. TRUMP
>
> You gotta do better than that, Doc. Can't lose focus.

> DOCTOR
>
> I want to hear your dream. Just tell me your dream.

> DONALD J. TRUMP
>
> Yes. In this dream I'm holding out my hands - *like we're doing now* - but my small fists are closed. Clenched shut. Like I'm trying to hide something from myself in one of my hands. Not sure which hand yet. And for the longest time I stare at both hands and finally I pick the one I think is concealing something. And when I open it - you won't believe this - when I unclench my fists there's a tiny miniature version of my father inside.

> DOCTOR
>
> What's he doing?

> DONALD J. TRUMP
>
> He is dressed the way he always was…crisp pinstriped suit with a bit of cracked dirt on his shoes from visiting all those nasty construction sites. And he's holding out his hands just like I'm doing now. Fists balled up. And again I have to pick one. And when I do there's another *even*

smaller version of me this time, inside *his* hands, again holding out *my* hands, with another even tinier version of him. And so it goes. A smaller version of me revealing a smaller version of him. Each one of us balled up in each other's fist. Until I'm so small that the size of my hands becomes totally irrelevant, as my father and I continue to conceal and reveal smaller and smaller versions of each other....

DOCTOR
How long does this go on...?

DONALD J. TRUMP
It's like a hall of mirrors. Smaller and smaller and smaller... until finally I *CLAP* my hands shut. Just to stop from disappearing. And although I love the sound of applause - this sounds more like a *yuuuge* bomb going off... something almost *nuclear*... but it's also the best applause I've ever heard. Like the entire world was clapping for me all at the same time. A mushroom cloud of love rising from my father's closed punishing hands.

Trump dramatically smacks his hands resoundingly together.

DONALD J. TRUMP
Think it means anything?

He and Doctor regard each other in a stunned silence. What might resemble a tear, crawls out from Donald's eye.

TRANSPARENT FALSEHOOD

DOCTOR *(suddenly concerned)*
Not sure Donny, but maybe you should cut back on that hair tonic, could lower the blood pressure you know.

DONALD J. TRUMP
Nah I'm fine. I'm good.
(He turns to his Invisible Camera Crew.)
Isn't that right guys…?

Doctor looks around, sees nobody there.

DOCTOR
Who are you talking to?

DONALD J. TRUMP
My camera crew.

DOCTOR
They're here?

DONALD J. TRUMP
All around us…. don't you see them?

Doctor looks about puzzled and concerned.

8

AS YOUR MOST INTERESTING SUBJECT AND PRESIDENT

Scene: Trump paces the empty Oval Office in his bathrobe. Back and forth, practicing Russian phrases on Google Translate. Followed by his Invisible Film Crew.

TV in background features Comey and others testifying before Mueller.

> DONALD J. TRUMP
> Show me the money. Show me the money!
> *(Google translates phonetically and he repeats)*
> Pokazhi mne den'gi! Pokazhi mne den'gi!

He picks up a putter, putts a golf ball across the carpet.

> DONALD J. TRUMP
> Show. Me. The. Money. *(in bad Russian)* Pokazhi. Mne. Den'gi!

He shuts off Comey's TV testimony, then crosses to retrieve golf ball. Trips. Turns to accuse the Invisible Camera Crew.

DONALD J. TRUMP

Jesus! Watch where you're going! If you're going to follow me around you've got to stay out of my way. You don't want to be tripping your subject. Not very professional!

He struggles to get up.

DONALD J. TRUMP

-What?!
- I don't look like a Russian bear. Who said that?
- No. I don't sound like one either.

Trump finally extends his hand for someone to help him up.

DONALD J. TRUMP

Go on. What are you waiting for? Help "the bear" up.

But soon as he touches the invisible hand, he cries out. And immediately drops back down to floor.

DONALD J. TRUMP

- Ouch!! You gave me a shock. You shocked me on purpose!
- Yes you did!
- Of course you're real. How else would I get shocked? How?!

He struggles up on his own. Waves golf club about.

DONALD J. TRUMP
Don't touch me. Give me some room. You guys are always too close. Stay back. No more shocks!

He resumes pacing and putting - taking some wide turns to avoid the crew at his heels.

DONALD J. TRUMP
Pokazhi mne den'gi! Pokazhi mne den'gi!

He stops.

DONALD J. TRUMP
- What? What did you say now?
- Don't lie to me. I heard you!
- Of course I paid you! Are you accusing the President of the United States of not paying his debts?
- Then what exactly are you saying…?
- That's what I thought. Because as your most famous and interesting subject *you* should probably be paying *me*. Losers! You know what this can do for your careers? How often do you get an opportunity like this?
- Come on. It's 4 in the morning. You can't just quit. Give me a break. You'll get paid soon as I get mine from Rosneft. I promise you. Even if I go to jail, you'll get paid. Once the banks open, you'll get your blood money. Donald J. Trump always delivers on his promises. Oh wait! Here.

He runs across room and removes a Renoir painting from the Wall.

DONALD J. TRUMP

Here! Take this as collateral. *(Pause)* What do you mean it's fake?! This is worth millions! *Millions!* Forget it. What do you guys know about art anyway. Nothing. Just point your cameras and shoot. Shit isn't even scripted.

He crosses to an armchair and drops in it. His bathrobe flays open, exposing his wizened genitals. He closes his robe, concealing his privates from the Camera.

DONALD J. TRUMP

Something very strange happened to me the other night. Very telling. Might have been a dream, but I'm not so sure. I couldn't sleep. And so I went out into the moonlight, stroll in the Rose Garden, clear my head, lungs. But just as I turned to go back in... this COYOTE - *fuck if I know where it came from!* - suddenly appeared and followed me back into the White House. Quietly. Stealthily. I didn't even know it was there. Very sneaky. Coyotes. So sneaky and quiet that even the Secret Service missed him. Which is why I'm hoping you guys got it on film. Well, this coyote snuck behind me back into the White House and into the Oval Office. And just waited there silently for me to turn around. Very stealthy. When I finally did, its teeth were all sharp and bared, growling at me. Just me and him there, in the dead of the night, middle of the Oval Office. Can't get more scary than that! Know what I did...? *(Slight dramatic pause.)* I growled back. GRRRR!! And I kept growling. *Grrrrr! You know who I am?!!* I shouted. *Who you're fucking with here,* I asked? *This is the president of the most powerful country in the world!* At which point El Coyote stopped his growling and slunk sheepishly to the corner and curled up. And at that moment - at that precise moment - I knew this feral coyote would be the First Family Dog. Not like Sunny, that sad neutered Portuguese water dog the Obama's had. But something wild that I personally domesticated and made my own. But in the morning… in the morning he was gone and I wasn't sure if it was all a dream or not. Was it all in my head? *(He snorts from a small vial.)* Am I really still the President…? Because none of it seems to make sense, not without the footage. I need to see the footage pronto!

All at once a loud clatter sounds from the other end of the room, followed by some ominous knocking.

DONALD J. TRUMP
What?! Already? No. Too soon. Too soon. *(To Camera Crew)* Quick. Go away. Hide. Do your little Ninja thing.

DONALD J. TRUMP
Hello? Who's there?

Out of the shadows, a Figure materializes sitting at the Oval Desk.

It's dressed in KKK regalia - White Robe and White Pointed Hood.

ROBED FIGURE
Don't you know who I am?

TRANSPARENT FALSEHOOD

DONALD J. TRUMP
Dad…?

DAD
Am I that hard to recognize?

DONALD J. TRUMP
It's been a while. What are you doing here?

DAD
Aren't you happy to see me?

DONALD J. TRUMP
I thought you were —

DAD *(overlapping)*
Shhh!

Dad removes his White Pointed KKK Hood.

DAD
Get's hot under this thing.

DONALD J. TRUMP
You look good dad. Considering.

DAD
Made it from Obama's besmirched bedsheets. Hahaha. Not bad. Had to bribe the housekeeper. But it was worth it.

DONALD J. TRUMP
Are you even real…?

DAD

More real than your camera crew. You want, you can touch my hand and I'll give you another shock.

DONALD J. TRUMP

No!

DAD

What's wrong? I've never seen you this scared.

DONALD J. TRUMP

I'm not scared. I just don't like getting shocked.

DAD

Of course not. *Who does? (Beat)* You might want to get rid of the bathrobe. Put on some clothes.

DONALD J. TRUMP

Why are you here, Dad? They sent you to fire me…?

DAD

Do you *want* me to fire you?

DONALD J. TRUMP

I tried to fire myself once, you know. Just to see if I could do it. Kept staring into the mirror, looking really serious, saying, *You're fired! YOU'RE FIRED!!* But I just couldn't do it.

DAD

You want me to help, I can?

DONALD J. TRUMP
Nah. I'm President dad. Can you believe it? Me...? *PRESIDENT!*

DAD
They say you were helped by the Russians, is that true?

DONALD J. TRUMP
No, Dad. Of course not! I mean you should've seen the inauguration. They say it was the biggest one ever. You'd have been so proud. This job, Dad, is so much harder than *Celebrity Apprentice*. The people I've had to fire. You won't believe it. Attorney General, FBI director, National Security Advisor, Communications Advisor, Personal Advisor, Chief of Staff. So many high profile departures.

DAD
Don't forget Rex, son.

DONALD J. TRUMP
Ha! Who's the moron now? *(Trump looks at him.)* But how did you-

DAD
We get your tweets where I am. It's the only pleasure they grant us.

DONALD J. TRUMP
Good, because there's going to be plenty more of these "high profile departures" by the time I'm done. Losers! Now they want to put me in jail. People get so jealous. But I won. I'm the President even if they take me away.

           DAD
Anything's better than that *shvartze* in the White House.

           DONALD J. TRUMP
Mirror mirror on the wall, who's the whitest President of All…?

           DAD
Sometimes you make me so proud son.

           DONALD J. TRUMP
I'm going to make big changes, Dad. Repeal all regulations for banks, businesses, and the environment. Fuck climate change! I'm gonna rewrite the Constitution and dedicate it to *you* Dad. I'm gonna make America great again!

           DAD
We're all rooting for you down here. But can I give you a little advice?

           DONALD J. TRUMP
Sure dad. Sure.

           DAD
You should be more careful.

Peremptory KNOCK on door.

           DONALD J. TRUMP *(shouting off)*
I'll be out when I'm ready!

DAD
At some point the mess will catch up with you, son. It always does. You can't keep shifting the goal posts forever.

DONALD J. TRUMP
Why not?

DAD
This isn't a simple case of mortgaging out early. I had to go in front of the Housing Commission, and let me tell you, it wasn't fun.

More KNOCKING.

DONALD J. TRUMP
I said WHEN READY!!
(Knocking stops.)
I can always pardon myself if I have to. Much easier than firing, I'm sure.

DAD *(all at once earnest)*
What about me, son? Will you be pardoning your poor old dad…?

DONALD J. TRUMP
I'm not sure these things work down where you are.

DAD
You can always try. *Indulgences* are a funny thing.

DONALD J. TRUMP
Actually, I might need them all for myself. Or for Donald Jr. Boy keeps getting himself in trouble, one mess after another.

More KNOCKING. Donald throws cell phone at door. It stops.

DONALD J. TRUMP
See what I have to deal with, Dad?! Those Hillary loving bastards all want to crucify me! Just because I'm trying to protect my family. It's amazing how much ugliness and hate there is in this world. Sad. Ugly. Failing planet earth. When I lie, at least you know it's *the truth* I'm lying about. Not like them.
  (He notices that his Dad is jotting stuff in his Little Black Book.)
What the hell are you writing down? My whole childhood you wrote things down. Credit/ Debit. Secret numbers. What did you just write down?

DAD
Nothing....

DONALD J. TRUMP
Tell me.

DAD
You'll find out when you get here.

DONALD J. TRUMP
I want to see. Now!

Donald grabs it. And reads in disbelief.

    DONALD J. TRUMP *(flipping pages)*
TRUMP TRUMP TRUMP TRUMP TRUMP... That it?

    DAD *(sadly apologetic)*
So I won't forget. At your age I already started to forget things... everything became more distant... *elusive.* Thoughts, words, feelings.

    DONALD J. TRUMP
I'm not like that.

    DAD
Not yet.

    DONALD J. TRUMP
I'll never get like that, dad. NEVER!!

    DAD
Anger was the last thing to go before you become a child again. Angry that you can't even recall your own Christian name. *Trump, Trump Trump...*

    DONALD J. TRUMP
That's why I'm putting it everywhere now. On every building. Every golf course. Jackson's 20 Dollar bill. Not some little black notebook. Or pissing it in the melting snow.

    DAD *(simultaneous/underneath)*
Trump Trump Trump Trump...

DONALD J. TRUMP *(overlapping)*
I'm putting my name and face everywhere so I don't even need to be there to remember it. That's the beauty of what I do. My *stable genius*. To rebrand the lies as shining truth. Because how we remember things is all that matters.

DAD *(simultaneous/underneath)*
Trump Trump Trump Trump...

DONALD J. TRUMP *(overlapping)*
The Donald offers people the opportunity to believe in their unspoken dreams. These poor and broken people. While they dream of kissing Miss Universe on the lips, I'm raping them from behind with my lies. And I learned all this at a very early age. From *you* daddy. Thank you. When you took me to work on all your projects - and showed me how to renovate old buildings cheaply and like shit, but so that they still looked all shiny and new from the outside. Funny how very few coats of paint it takes to conceal the ugliness underneath.

DAD
You learned well, son. I schooled you well. But there's *still* one more thing you need to know.

More KNOCKING on door.

DONALD J. TRUMP
No, Dad. Not now.

DAD
Are you afraid?

DONALD J. TRUMP
I need to get ready for my interview. You have to go.

DAD
You can't just make me disappear like your imaginary film crew.

DONALD J. TRUMP
They're not imaginary!! Guys, come out. Come out and introduce yourself to my dad.

DAD
There's no one there, Donny. No one. Maybe everyone else has been too afraid to tell you this. But not me.

DONALD J. TRUMP *(more desperate)*
Paul! Clive! Come on you guys.

Beat. No one responds.

DAD
You always had to be seen to exist. Always.

DONALD J. TRUMP
Ratings are important, Dad.

DAD
Of course. But you… you're obsessed.

More KNOCKING at door.

> DONALD J. TRUMP *(panicked)*
> What do you want, Dad? I don't have time for this. What do you want?!

> DAD
> Baby going to cry?

> DONALD J. TRUMP
> I won't let you do to me what you did to my brother. I'm not Fred.

> DAD
> Oh please, your brother was weak. Sensitive. Not like you, Donny. So strong. Arrogant. *Hateful!!*

> DONALD J. TRUMP
> You're making fun of me.

> DAD
> Imagine if there was no one in the world to see you but me, Donny. Just me. As… you… are.

> DONALD J. TRUMP
> What are you talking about?

> DAD
> You'll never get rid of me. Even when I'm not here I'll be here. I'll always see you.

> DONALD J. TRUMP *(tantrum)*
> Go away. Go away. GO AWAY!

He breaks down, crying.

> DAD
> Here, here. Come sit on Daddy's lap.

KNOCKING on Door resumes. Trump ignores it.

> VOICE (O.S.)
> Mr. President…?

Donny nuzzles closer against his father, absently reaching under his dad's shirt, as if looking for a breast to suck. Dad suddenly realizes what's happening, shocked.

> DAD
> Ewww! What are you doing?!

> DONALD J. TRUMP
> Nothing.

> DAD
> Keep your hands to yourself. You disgust me! What the hell's wrong with you?

He brusquely shoves Donald off his lap, wipes off his trousers.

> DONALD J. TRUMP
> Please daddy, I'm sorry. Just hold me. Don't ever leave me.

GIL KOFMAN

KNOCKING on Door resumes. Trump ignores it.

                    VOICE (O.S.)
Mr. President, we don't want to keep the Committee waiting.

Father extends his hands before him, towards Donald, palms upturned. Donald crawls towards him on floor. The old game in play

                        DAD
Come on, then. Rest your hands on mine. Let's see what you've really learned, Mr President. Let's see how good you really are. Playing against a dead old man. I'll bet the whole entire world you still can't beat me.

Father holds out his hands. Waits. Trump tentatively rests his hands in his Father's open palms. Beat. Who's going to make the first move...?

Another KNOCK on the door.

Lights Fade. Followed by a large atomic explosion of slapping hands.

END OF PLAY

AFTERWORD: THE TIMES THEY ARE A-CHANGIN (WAY TOO FAST)

Trump wasn't supposed to win; mercifully, I was never going to think about him ever again once the elections were over. But the cosmos had its own agenda — and once this putative president assumed his throne, I knew I had to put aside my other, more elegiac work (a play on English photographer Eadweard Muybidge) and focus on the chaos (euphemistic for disaster) unfolding all around me.

But where to start? How do you engage a subject whose audacity outstrips the imagination? Trump thrived on chaos; his campaign was a veritable Ponzi scheme of lies, old and new, that were often recycled from top to bottom, and resurrected back up again, from bottom to top, once the older exhumed lies had a chance to catch their breath. The audacity of Hope was now replaced with the mendacity of the Shameless, and nothing I could write would ever match the sheer invention of this man's inveterate and colorful corruption; a heedless unscrupulousness, as uncaring as it was poignantly un-self-aware. As if overnight, we were transported into a new Dark Age where facts were summarily banished and replaced with patently self-serving lies.

Now, it's hard enough for a writer to respectfully render reality. But to somehow compete with a fabricated universe of fraud and unfounded lies seemed beyond daunting. How do you construct a play about something so protean that it changes daily — nay, hourly; something so inconstant and balefully unpredictable that it defies narrative as we know it? Unlike the stock market, which hysterically twitched and quivered, in response to each and every one of Trump's galvanic and thoughtless whims, I was determined to find a more steadfast and reliable way to tell my story. Here I was, trying to write something to express my visceral disgust at Trump and his White House, and all the time the cast of characters kept changing, pulling focus from one set of depraved understudies to the next. Worse yet, my main protagonist was not only incapable of learning his lines, or sticking to one story, his consistently unreliable character insisted on going off-book to promulgate ego-driven, improvisatory riffs that only further reflected his own insecurities. More than once, I confess, I found myself humming a slightly demented version of a song from *The Sound of Music:*

> *How do you solve a problem like Trump?*
> *How do you catch a cloud and pin it down?*
> *How do you find a word that means Trump?*
> *A flibbertijibbet! A will-o'-the wisp! A clown!*

But I persevered. So strongly and stubbornly did I feel the need to expose this prevaricator in his own shape-shifting element, that I staunchly kept searching for a structure to accommodate and sustain all his unnerving and disorienting contradictions without capitulating to his rules. At all cost I had to somehow distill the essence of Trump and his toxicity before he succeeded to poison me and my sensibilities.

Without reverting to overly clever satire or ephemeral one-liners — which *Saturday Night Live* and the late-night shows splendidly provide — I wanted to create something about Trump that could live outside and, in fact, beyond him. Something durable, not disposable, like him and his sadly Manichean win-or-lose worldview. Only that could serve as my revenge: a work of mystery about someone who defied, denied and defiled all metaphor and mystery. A man whose only true romance is with lying itself.

So I worked and struggled to divine a flicker of art in the artless soul of Trump. Initially I was shocked and bedazzled by the unremitting and sensational outpouring of current events. But something instinctually told me to avoid this overt and incessant political bombardment, and to focus instead on a more private, contained Trump. A smaller, more manageable Trump, caught outside the public sphere and the bluster of politics, yet still consistent with — almost derived from — everything we've come to know of The Donald through his tireless media circus. Presently I found myself writing and inventing "outtakes of humanity" for a man who I thought had none. A document he would no doubt detest.

So now the play was writing itself: Trump putting Barron to bed; Trump preparing to go out for the night with Melania; Trump attending Parent's Day at school; Trump having Seder at Mar-a-Lago. Naturally, the politics of the outside world would now and again impinge itself upon the play and necessitate rewrites, but these touch-ups often had a short shelf life as they were invariably replaced by more urgent, shocking news like a passing summer storm. Yet the bedrock of the play held fast.

The first draft of *Transparent Falsehood: An American Travesty* finished, I now felt compelled to put it on. I've always thought that the role of theater was to be an exigent sounding board for what happens around us. Theater is immediate; more than the other arts, it lends itself to a kind of living analysis, a social vivisection. It is a breathing organism that communes with subject and spectator alike, and always in present time, not in a mediated form. Given all that was transpiring in the world, it seemed urgent to get this particular piece produced and seen — not as simple agitprop, but as legitimate theater attuned to the turbulence around it. Here finally was a play, imperfect as it may be, that in many ways was more presumptuously finished than the world it hopes to depict, a wishful stage for what might one day unfold, both pre-cautionary and woeful.

www.ingramcontent.com/pod-product-compliance
Lightning Source LLC
LaVergne TN
LVHW051522070426
835507LV00023B/3256